Learning from Our Mistakes: Difficulties and Failures in Feminist Therapy

Learning from Our Mistakes: Difficulties and Failures in Feminist Therapy has been co-published simultaneously as *Women & Therapy,* Volume 21, Number 3 1998.

Learning from Our Mistakes: Difficulties and Failures in Feminist Therapy

Marcia Hill, EdD
Esther D. Rothblum, PhD
Editors

Learning from Our Mistakes: Difficulties and Failures in Feminist Therapy has been co-published simultaneously as *Women & Therapy,* Volume 21, Number 3 1998.

The Haworth Press, Inc.
New York • London

Learning from Our Mistakes: Difficulties and Failures in Feminist Therapy has been co-published simultaneously as *Women & Therapy,* ™ Volume 21, Number 3 1998.

The development, preparation, and publication of this work has been undertaken with great care. However, the publisher, employees, editors, and agents of The Haworth Press and all imprints of The Haworth Press, Inc., including The Haworth Medical Press® and Pharmaceutical Products Press®, are not responsible for any errors contained herein or for consequences that may ensue from use of materials or information contained in this work. Opinions expressed by the author(s) are not necessarily those of The Haworth Press, Inc.

The Haworth Press, Inc., 10 Alice Street, Binghamton, NY 13904-1580 USA

Cover design by Thomas J. Mayshock Jr.

Library of Congress Cataloging-in-Publication Data

Learning from our mistakes : difficulties and failures in feminist therapy / Marcia Hill, Esther D. Rothblum, editors.
    p. cm.
    "Learning from our mistakes : difficulties and failures in feminist therapy has been co-published simultaneously as Women & therapy, Volume 21, Number 3, 1998."
    Includes bibliographical references and index.
    ISBN 0-7890-0653-7 (alk. paper). -- ISBN 0-7890-0670-7 (alk. paper)
    1. Feminist therapy. 2. Women and psychoanalysis. I. Hill, Marcia. II. Rothblum, Esther D.

RC489.F45L43 1998
616.89'14'082–dc21
                                            98-35594
                                             CIP

INDEXING & ABSTRACTING

Contributions to this publication are selectively indexed or abstracted in print, electronic, online, or CD-ROM version(s) of the reference tools and information services listed below. This list is current as of the copyright date of this publication. See the end of this section for additional notes.

- *Abstracts of Research in Pastoral Care & Counseling*, Loyola College, 7135 Minstrel Way, Suite 101, Columbia, MD 21045

- *Academic Abstracts/CD-ROM*, EBSCO Publishing Editorial Department, P.O. Box 590, Ipswich, MA 01938-0590

- *Academic Index (on-line)*, Information Access Company, 362 Lakeside Drive, Foster City, CA 94404

- *Alternative Press Index*, Alternative Press Center, Inc., P.O. Box 33109, Baltimore, MD 21218-0401

- *Behavioral Medicine Abstracts*, University of Washington, Department of Social Work & Speech & Hearing Sciences, Box 354900, Seattle, WA 98195

- *CNPIEC Reference Guide: Chinese National Directory of Foreign Periodicals*, P.O. Box 88, Beijing, People's Republic of China

- *Contemporary Women's Issues,* Responsive Databases Services, 23611 Chagrin Blvd., Suite 320, Beachwood, OH 44122

- *Current Contents: Clinical Medicine/Life Sciences (CC: CM/LS) (weekly Table of Contents Service), and Social Science Citation Index. Articles also searchable through Social SciSearch, ISI's online database and in ISI's Research Alert current awareness service*, Institute for Scientific Information, 3501 Market Street, Philadelphia, PA 19104-3302 (USA)

- *Digest of Neurology and Psychiatry*, The Institute of Living, 400 Washington Street, Hartford, CT 06106

- *Expanded Academic Index,* Information Access Company, 362 Lakeside Drive, Forest City, CA 94404

- *Family Studies Database (online and CD/ROM),* National Information Services Corporation, 306 East Baltimore Pike, 2nd Floor, Media, PA 19063

(continued)

- *Family Violence & Sexual Assault Bulletin*, Family Violence & Sexual Assault Institute, 1121 E. South East Loop 323, Suite 130, Tyler, TX 75701
- *Feminist Periodicals: A Current Listing of Contents*, Women's Studies Librarian-at-Large, 728 State Street, 430 Memorial Library, Madison, WI 53706
- *Health Source: Indexing & Abstracting of 160 selected health related journals, updated monthly:* EBSCO Publishing, 83 Pine Street, Peabody, MA 01960
- *Health Source Plus: expanded version of "Health Source" to be released shortly:* EBSCO Publishing, 83 Pine Street, Peabody, MA 01960
- *Higher Education Abstracts*, Claremont Graduate University, 231 East Tenth Street, Claremont, CA 91711
- *IBZ International Bibliography of Periodical Literature*, Zeller Verlag GmbH & Co., P.O.B. 1949, d-49009, Osnabruck, Germany
- *Index to Periodical Articles Related to Law*, University of Texas, 727 East 26th Street, Austin, TX 78705
- *INTERNET ACCESS (& additional networks) Bulletin Board for Libraries ("BUBL") coverage of information resources on INTERNET, JANET, and other networks.*
  - <URL:http://bubl.ac.uk/>
  - The new locations will be found under <URL:http://bubl.ac.uk/link/>.
  - Any existing BUBL users who have problems finding information on the new service should contact the BUBL help line by sending e-mail to <bubl@bubl.ac.uk>.
  The Andersonian Library, Curran Building, 101 St. James Road, Glasgow G4 0NS, Scotland
- *Mental Health Abstracts (online through DIALOG)*, IFI/Plenum Data Company, 3202 Kirkwood Highway, Wilmington, DE 19808
- *ONS Nursing Scan in Oncology-NAACOG's Women's Health Nursing Scan*, NURSECOM, Inc., 1211 Locust Street, Philadelphia, PA 19107
- *PASCAL, c/o Institute de L'Information Scientifique et Technique. Cross-disciplinary electronic database covering the fields of science, technology & medicine.* Also available on CD-ROM, and can generate customized retrospective searches. For more information: INIST, Customer Desk, 2, allee du Parc de Brabois, F-54514 Vandoeuvre Cedex, France; http//www.inist.fr

(continued)

- *Periodical Abstracts, Research I* (general & basic reference indexing & abstracting data-base from University Microfilms International (UMI), 300 North Zeeb Road, P.O. Box 1346, Ann Arbor, MI 48106-1346), UMI Data Courier, P.O. Box 32770, Louisville, KY 40232-2770

- *Periodical Abstracts, Research II* (broad coverage indexing & abstracting data-base from University Microfilms International (UMI), 300 North Zeeb Road, P.O. Box 1346, Ann Arbor, MI 48106-1346), UMI Data Courier, P.O. Box 32770, Louisville, KY 40232-2770

- *Psychological Abstracts (PsycINFO)*, American Psychological Association, P.O. Box 91600, Washington, DC 20090-1600

- *Published International Literature on Traumatic Stress (The PILOTS Database)*, National Center for Post-Traumatic Stress Disorder (116D), VA Medical Center, White River Junction, VT 05009

- *Sage Family Studies Abstracts (SFSA)*, Sage Publications, Inc., 2455 Teller Road, Newbury Park, CA 91320

- *Social Work Abstracts*, National Association of Social Workers, 750 First Street NW, 8th Floor, Washington, DC 20002

- *Sociological Abstracts (SA),* Sociological Abstracts, Inc., P.O. Box 22206, San Diego, CA 92192-0206

- *Studies on Women Abstracts*, Carfax Publishing Company, P.O. Box 25, Abingdon, Oxon OX14 3UE, United Kingdom

- *Violence and Abuse Abstracts: A Review of Current Literature on Interpersonal Violence (VAA)*, Sage Publications, Inc., 2455 Teller Road, Newbury Park, CA 91320

- *Women "R" CD/ROM*, Softline Information, Inc., 20 Summer Street, Stamford, CT 06901. A new full text Windows Database on CD/ROM. Presents full depth coverage of the wide range of subjects that impact and reflect the lives of women. Can be reached at 1 (800) 524-7922, www.slinfo.com, or e-mail: hoch@slinfo.com

- *Women Studies Abstracts*, Rush Publishing Company, P.O. Box 1, Rush, NY 14543

- *Women's Studies Index (indexed comprehensively)*, G. K. Hall & Co., P.O. Box 159, Thorndike, ME 04986

(continued)

SPECIAL BIBLIOGRAPHIC NOTES

related to special journal issues (separates)
and indexing/abstracting

☐ indexing/abstracting services in this list will also cover material in any "separate" that is co-published simultaneously with Haworth's special thematic journal issue or DocuSerial. Indexing/abstracting usually covers material at the article/chapter level.

☐ monographic co-editions are intended for either non-subscribers or libraries which intend to purchase a second copy for their circulating collections.

☐ monographic co-editions are reported to all jobbers/wholesalers/approval plans. The source journal is listed as the "series" to assist the prevention of duplicate purchasing in the same manner utilized for books-in-series.

☐ to facilitate user/access services all indexing/abstracting services are encouraged to utilize the co-indexing entry note indicated at the bottom of the first page of each article/chapter/contribution.

☐ this is intended to assist a library user of any reference tool (whether print, electronic, online, or CD-ROM) to locate the monographic version if the library has purchased this version but not a subscription to the source journal.

☐ individual articles/chapters in any Haworth publication are also available through the Haworth Document Delivery Service (HDDS).

Learning from Our Mistakes: Difficulties and Failures in Feminist Therapy

CONTENTS

ABOUT THE EDITORS

Marcia Hill, EdD, is a psychologist who has spent over 20 years practicing psychotherapy. She is Co-Editor of the journal *Women & Therapy* and a member and past Chair of the Feminist Therapy Institute. In addition to therapy, Dr. Hill does occasional teaching, writing, and consulting in the areas of feminist therapy theory and practice. The Editor of *More than a Mirror: How Clients Influence Therapists' Lives* (1997) and *Feminist Therapy as a Political Act* (1998), she has co-edited four other Haworth books: *Classism and Feminist Therapy: Counting Costs* (1996); *Couples Therapy: Feminist Perspectives* (1996); *Children's Rights, Therapists' Responsibilities: Feminist Commentaries* (1997); and *Breaking the Rules: Women in Prison and Feminist Therapy* (1998). She is currently in private practice in Montpelier, Vermont.

Esther D. Rothblum, PhD, is Professor in the Department of Psychology at the University of Vermont. She was the recipient of a Kellogg Fellowship that involved travel to Africa to study women's mental health. Her research and writing have focused on mental health disorders in which women predominate, including depression, the social stigma of women's weight, procrastination and fear of failure, and women in the Antarctic. She has co-edited 21 books, including *Another Silenced Trauma: Twelve Feminist Therapists and Activists Respond to One Woman's Recovery from War,* which won a Distinguished Publication Award from the Association for Women in Psychology.

Concerning Failure

Marcia Hill

A businessman once remarked to me that the traditional way of paying for therapy was like paying to have a house built by the brick. I replied that if we used that analogy, then it would also mean that the builder/therapist would be in the position of having the blueprints changed several times in mid-project, of having little idea how many workers would show up on any given day, and of being beset by occasional natural disasters that wiped out some of the work already accomplished. And that is even before we try to factor in the general skill and experience of the builder or her expertise with the particular kind of house the client wants.

Given the unpredictability of that scenario, it's difficult to know how to think about those therapies that do not go well. To think that even an ideal therapist can succeed with every client insults the power of the client and implies therapist omnipotence. Conversely, assuming that an ideally motivated client can succeed with any therapist–or, put differently, that all failure is resistance–is a convenient excuse to duck therapist responsibility. Sometimes the most talented of therapists and the most motivated of clients are simply poorly matched; sometimes an uncertain client and a marginally skilled therapist find a chemistry together that produces magic. Sometimes there is nothing to point to but the limits of knowledge or, as Nanette Gartrell reminds us, the limits of the nature of therapy itself.

Even my generalizations here about therapist and client have layers and layers of complexity. A motivated client is willing to be affected by therapy, to bring the self as fully as possible to the exchange, to continue struggling outside of the therapy hour. A skilled therapist, beyond the textbook givens of empathy and technique, has a certain presence, a will-

[Haworth co-indexing entry note]: "Concerning Failure." Hill, Marcia. Co-published simultaneously in *Women & Therapy* (The Haworth Press, Inc.) Vol. 21, No. 3, 1998, pp. 1-3; and: *Learning from Our Mistakes: Difficulties and Failures in Feminist Therapy* (ed: Marcia Hill and Esther D. Rothblum) The Haworth Press, Inc., 1998, pp. 1-3. Single or multiple copies of this article are available for a fee from The Haworth Document Delivery Service [1-800-342-9678, 9:00 a.m. - 5:00 p.m. (EST). E-mail address: getinfo@haworthpressinc.com].

1

ingness to take risks, a knack for guessing right and offering each client the options that fit. With each layer of these meanings comes the possibility of inadequacy, of a bad match. And let's not forget the elements of luck and timing. For example, a client may want badly to stop smoking, but if the timing coincides with too many life stresses, her chances of success are not that great. And we have all known the remarkable experience of plodding along with a client when some life happenstance suddenly coalesces months of effort or opens doors in precisely the right way, and we're left wondering whether therapy can be credited for much of the change at all.

Adding to the confusion, defining success in therapy is elusive at best. Sometimes people seek help for fairly encapsulated concerns, and it is relatively easy to judge whether the worrisome symptom has abated. But for many it's not that straightforward. Even when the client and I agree that we've accomplished a lot, how much of that is a covert agreement to avoid cognitive dissonance? I know I have in some situations thought that all was well and completed work with someone, only to hear later through the grapevine that the client had sought another therapist for the same difficulties, suggesting that if I helped at all, it was limited. I have also thought with some people that I was of little use to them, only to hear later what a difference I made in their lives. I suspect that therapists' definitions of good therapy and those of clients may be divergent more often than we guess. I once heard this described as "the prejudice of depth," i.e., the clinician's inclination to think that "deep" therapy is the only good therapy, when clients may not experience anything of the sort.

In college I once watched a movie about birth defects, all the things that can go wrong in the immensely complicated process of conception, gestation and birth. I remember walking around the campus afterward being filled with astonishment at the sight of all those people for whom these hundreds of genetic and developmental details had mostly gone right. It seemed miraculous. Therapy is like that, too: hundreds of moments in every session in which the client could despair, the therapist might injure. And, let's face it, none of us are that ideal therapist; our clients, as well, are mortals only. Yet, research continues to show that most therapies go well enough to be considered helpful by the client as well as the therapist. I imagine each of us, client and therapist, accommodating and forgiving one another from moment to moment in a mutual effort to build something worthwhile, to make a home that the client can live in comfortably.

Listen, then, to these stories and musings of discouragement and confusion and even failure. Consider the piece on ethics, which offers a model for thinking through some kinds of difficulties with clients. Weigh for yourself the speculations of Jeanne Adleman, Marny Hall, and Natalie Porter as they reflect on the problem of failure in therapy. I like to think that with each client I become a bit better therapist, learning from my observations and from what works and from my mistakes. The literature is full of the encouragement of what works; here we turn our attention to the aspect of education that most of us do more privately: grappling with our uncertainties and inadequacies. It may be that there is more to be learned from our errors, and those of our colleagues who have been willing to risk disclosure in this volume, than from our own and others' successes. At the very least, in opening a conversation about failures and difficulties in therapy, I hope that each of us can feel less alone, and that we can learn together from our mistakes.

A Case of Eroticized Transference

Nanette K. Gartrell

SUMMARY. The author discusses her work with a client who experienced an obsessional, eroticized transference. Various strategies for containing the treatment are presented. An independent evaluator recommended that the client transfer her care to another provider. The pros and cons of terminating with this client are discussed. *[Article copies available for a fee from The Haworth Document Delivery Service: 1-800-342-9678. E-mail address: getinfo@haworthpressinc.com]*

Sometimes I fantasize that erotic transference has built-in age limits. I imagine that I will no longer be the object of clients' eroticized feelings in my senior years, and therefore will be spared the challenge of handling this prickly clinical issue deftly and tactfully. I pretend that, in this one instance, ageism will work to my advantage. Invariably, my reveries end with assorted reminders that transference is unconscious, fanciful, and timeless. It amuses me to recall my first encounter with erotic fantasy in the context of therapy. A classmate had confided that she had a crush on

Nanette K. Gartrell, MD, is Associate Clinical Professor of Psychiatry at the University of California, San Francisco, where she teaches ethics and feminist psychotherapy theory. She has been documenting sexual abuse by physicians since 1982 and conducting a national longitudinal lesbian family study since 1986.

The author would like to thank Dee Mosbacher, Esther Rothblum, Jane Futcher, Jasna Stefanovic, Joan Biren, and Marny Hall for their assistance in the preparation of this manuscript.

Address correspondence to Dr. Gartrell at 3570 Clay Street, San Francisco, CA 94118.

[Haworth co-indexing entry note]: "A Case of Eroticized Transference." Gartrell, Nanette K. Co-published simultaneously in *Women & Therapy* (The Haworth Press, Inc.) Vol. 21, No. 3, 1998, pp. 5-11; and: *Learning from Our Mistakes: Difficulties and Failures in Feminist Therapy* (ed: Marcia Hill and Esther D. Rothblum) The Haworth Press, Inc., 1998, pp. 5-11. Single or multiple copies of this article are available for a fee from The Haworth Document Delivery Service [1-800-342-9678, 9:00 a.m. - 5:00 p.m. (EST). E-mail address: getinfo@haworthpressinc.com].

her therapist. She described him as a middle-aged man who had the "most gorgeous curly brown hair and deep-set eyes." Several weeks later, she pointed him out to me on campus. He was bald!

Although erotic transference often spices up therapy for the client, it has the opposite effect on me. I confess that my first inclination is to duck and cover when I see it coming. I always consult with colleagues when I encounter this dynamic, because I do not want my dislikes to affect the treatment adversely. My consultants have always advised me to stick it out with clients who develop intense erotic feelings toward me–to help them resolve their unconscious conflicts and progress to a healthier stage of relational development.

This concept of working through the transference (i.e., sticking it out indefinitely) was modified a few years ago when I treated a client who experienced an obsessional delusion. After she disclosed her feelings toward me, the client began to decompensate. None of my efforts to contain her were successful. My consultants ran out of suggestions. I felt frustrated and impotent. The client eventually agreed to an independent evaluation. The evaluator recommended that she terminate with me, and seek treatment with another therapist. When this client finally ended her work with me, I must admit I was relieved to see her go.

CASE REPORT[1]

Caitlin (a pseudonym) was a white, heterosexual, 36-year-old attorney who sought treatment with me to discuss unresolved issues concerning her mother's death two years previously. Caitlin had never been in therapy. She was the third of five siblings (two brothers and three sisters), a graduate of Ivy League schools, a partner in her firm, and the fiancée of a successful stockbroker. We spent the first several months of our weekly sessions focusing on her grief concerning her mother. Caitlin initially reported that she had a very loving family that had grown even closer during her mother's long illness; but over time, a different picture emerged. Caitlin never felt that she had been special to her mother, and, as a result, had considerable unresolved anger toward her mother. By moving home during her mother's final year, Caitlin had hoped they would develop a closer bond; but her mother had not been particularly appreciative. This was the topic of our discussions until one session when Caitlin's frustration with her fiancé's inattentiveness changed our focus from her

---

1. The facts in this account have been altered to conceal the client's identity.

grief to practical considerations. We spoke briefly of possible strategies for eliciting more support from him.

The following Sunday I opened my newspaper to find an envelope addressed to me. I did not recognize the handwriting. The enclosed note read:

> Dear Nanette, I am very disturbed about something that has been happening in our relationship. I had been feeling so supported by you, and now I feel that you have misled me. I hope you will call to discuss this with me as soon as possible. With best wishes, Caitlin

I was perplexed by the content of the note, and disturbed by Caitlin's method of delivery. I left her a voicemail message the following day, informing her that I had received her note, and that I would be glad to discuss its content during our next appointment two days hence.

Caitlin seemed slightly flustered when she arrived for our next appointment. She thanked me for calling her. She then explained that she thought I had been disappointed with her when I had encouraged her to be more assertive with her fiancé in our previous session. I explored her feeling. Caitlin said that she had been considering calling off their engagement. Because she had not discussed her relationship in much detail, I suggested that we defer that topic until our next appointment. I pointed out several times during the session that she changed the focus whenever we addressed her concerns about me. Before the session's end, I emphasized the importance of her sharing her feelings about me during our sessions–not by letter or telephone at a later time. I explained that I did not respond to communication between appointments unless there was an emergency. As she walked out of my office, Caitlin apologized for leaving the note.

Caitlin left a phone message two days later that she had something very important to discuss. Before I had a chance to consider my response, she left three additional messages, listing her various telephone numbers and reiterating the urgency of her need to speak with me. I returned her call later that day. Caitlin said that she had broken up with her fiancé. She did not sound at all distressed. After verifying that she was indeed coping adequately, I told her that I would discuss her decision during our next session. Caitlin left four more messages before our next appointment. She called to thank me for returning her calls, to tell me how she was doing, and to list topics for further discussion. I was beginning to feel apprehensive about the frequency of her calls. That concern prompted my first consultation with a colleague.

The consultant discussed several strategies for containing Caitlin's treatment within the therapy session. These included: (1) focusing on

Caitlin's fear of loss; (2) exploring the association between her anxiety and her phone calls; (3) encouraging Caitlin to keep a journal; and (4) suggesting that she record in her journal the feelings she'd like to discuss with me so that she could refresh her memory prior to our appointments.

Caitlin circumvented all the limits I set. Within several weeks, she was calling between 5 and 10 times per week. Initially, my office assistant fielded the calls. Caitlin figured out that she could bypass my assistant by stating that she was calling with an emergency. When I responded, she never sounded distressed; indeed, she sounded pleased to hear from me. She continued to behave politely and agreeably during our sessions. Typically, she sidestepped inquiries about her feelings for me and her motivations for communicating between appointments.

At one point, the frequency of her calls tripled. She left cryptic messages indicating that she had "something important" to tell me. Now, though, she was content to wait until our next appointment to disclose the details. In that session, Caitlin informed me that she was attracted to me.

I responded by saying that it was natural for her to feel that way, and that therapy sometimes elicits such feelings. I explained that I would never become sexually involved with a current or former client–that it would be unethical for any therapist to do so. I asked how she felt about my response. Caitlin said she felt relieved that I hadn't told her to "take a hike." She also said that she understood the legalities of doctor-client sex, and repeated that she respected my boundaries.

Her actual response to my limit-setting was to diversify her between-session contacts to include letters, notes, and flower deliveries, in addition to the phone calls. She told me that she was having difficulty focusing on her work because she was so preoccupied with me. Apparently, Caitlin spent most of each day hoping and waiting for a response from me. She also began showing up at events that she had guessed correctly I might attend.

By then I had begun to feel invaded and frustrated. Again, I consulted my colleague. We discussed various treatment strategies. One approach was to continue working with Caitlin's eroticized transference. If Caitlin understood that I could endure the intensity of her feelings, perhaps she would learn not to be ruled by them. Another idea was to acknowledge that we had reached a therapeutic impasse, and to recommend an independent evaluation (Elkind, 1992). I decided to pursue the latter–an approach that represented a radical departure from my training and customary practice.

In the next session with Caitlin, an opportunity arose for me to suggest her seeing an outside evaluator. I explained that clients sometimes seek independent consultations when they encounter unresolvable dilemmas in treatment (Elkind, 1992). Caitlin seemed relieved, and asked for several referrals. She scheduled an appointment with a colleague, and gave me permission to communicate with her.

In the course of the evaluation, Caitlin was asked if she were in love with me. Caitlin replied, "Yes." Caitlin also told the evaluator that I was legally prohibited from becoming sexually involved with clients, but that she was certain that I was in love with her, too. Believing that Caitlin's delusion might have borderline qualities, the evaluator was concerned that Caitlin might decompensate further if she continued in treatment with me. With that in mind, the evaluator recommended that Caitlin consider transferring her care to another therapist. The evaluator explained that Caitlin could benefit from a less charged therapy experience which would allow her to refocus on the topic that had brought her to treatment–grieving the loss of her mother.

Caitlin vacillated about terminating with me. She continued calling between 10 and 15 times per week. Even though I was feeling under siege and hoped she would transfer her care, I discussed both sides of her ambivalence. I tried to be patient and understanding when I met or spoke with her. I explored her options regarding other therapists. Finally, with a flurry of letters, she terminated.

I heard nothing from Caitlin for five months. During that time, I remained hypervigilant about mail and messages, because I was unconvinced that Caitlin would cease contact. When she called again, it was to complain that her new therapist had said that Caitlin had an inflated sense of her own importance in others' lives. Caitlin asked for my thoughts about this alleged feedback. I responded by letter that it was inappropriate for me to comment; I recommended that she discuss her feelings with her current therapist. Caitlin left a series of hostile messages in response to my letter. The angry messages were then followed by friendly, chatty messages. This pattern continues to this day. Her most recent message, conveyed in a very sweet tone, concluded: "I hope that life has *not* been treating you very well." It was unclear whether this was an unconscious misstatement.

DISCUSSION

It is difficult to know whether transferring Caitlin's care represented the best treatment option. Different schools of psychotherapy have varied perspectives on the management of delusional, obsessional clients. Some schools advocate a dynamic approach to the material evoked by the erotic transference. Others recommend liberal use of third-party consultation when it appears that a therapeutic impasse has been reached. My consultant and I felt that Caitlin had very little chance of returning to her former level of functioning as long as she maintained contact with me.

Nearly one quarter of clients with eroticized delusions develop their first obsession after a major loss (Evans, Jeckel, & Slott, 1982). Caitlin's transference could be interpreted as a pathological grief response to her mother's death. She was enraged that she had never felt special to her mother. Having failed to elicit the attention and appreciation she had sought during her mother's final hours, Caitlin's quest for love may have been transferred to the next important woman in her life–myself, her therapist. Whereas most clients who disclose feelings of attraction to therapists are able to respect professional boundaries, Caitlin's narcissism made it difficult for her to tolerate the limits I set. She experienced these boundaries as a recapitulation of her mother's unavailability.

Alternatively, Caitlin's obsession with me may represent a transitional step in her coming out process. Crushes on powerful, unattainable women (professors, coaches, mentors) often precede an acknowledgment of one's lesbianism. Healthier women move on from these crushes to more egalitarian lesbian relationships. Caitlin was obsessed with me, believed her feelings were reciprocated, and could not (or would not) respect my limits.

Despite my frustrations with Caitlin's behavior, I empathized with her pain. Witnessing her longing for greater closeness to me reminded me of my own unrequited loves. I recalled my various obsessions with powerful women whom I imagined might fill me up or complement me in some way. I revisited my own vulnerability to fixations on inappropriate, unattainable women at times of significant loss. Such vulnerability is a fairly universal experience. For most of us, it is also transitory.

Caitlin was unable or unwilling to relinquish her fantasy, and she was convinced that I shared her feelings. Confronting such an individual about the implausibility of such beliefs is rarely successful (Orion, 1997). If Caitlin had been able to work through her obsession while continuing in treatment with me, the toll on both of us would have been great. My life would have been severely disrupted, along with hers. Caitlin's willingness to transfer her care suggests that the recommendation was therapeutically sound.

I suspect that Caitlin's current therapist might also have felt frustrated with Caitlin, if, in fact, the therapist said anything close to what Caitlin conveyed to me five months after officially terminating with me. It was the kind of statement that might be made by a therapist whose countertransference irritation was not in check. I had vented my frustrations with a consultant in an effort to avoid acting them out in treatment. I wondered if the current therapist knew of Caitlin's work with me; I suspected not, as I had never been contacted for records or information.

Inevitably, cases like this raise the issue of terminating with a client before the therapeutic work is complete. I would have liked my work with Caitlin to have come to a more satisfactory conclusion. I regret not having the opportunity to facilitate Caitlin's healing around her mother's death. I am disappointed that she left in a more disorganized state than the one in which she arrived. Of some solace is Sue Elkind's reminder that "ruptured therapeutic relationships need not be conceived of as the consequence of a deficiency in patient or therapist or of an imperfect theory, but rather as the inevitable consequence of an intimate human relationship constructed to elicit areas of the patient's vulnerability" (p. 292).

It also took me longer than usual to recognize how disturbed Caitlin was, because she concealed her pathology behind an intelligent, sophisticated exterior. The independent evaluator found Caitlin "frightening." This evaluator also worries about becoming Caitlin's next target. Caitlin has continued to write and call her because she has been unable to obtain a response from me.

Perhaps someday Caitlin will develop more constructive outlets. In the meantime, I still feel guarded when I retrieve phone messages or open my mail. I scan the audience at public events. I shudder when I recall Caitlin's assertion that she was not the kind of person who would stalk me. I fantasize about a time when–having heard nothing from her for years–I can finally stamp her file "CASE CLOSED."

REFERENCES

Elkind, S.D. (1992). *Resolving impasses in therapeutic relationships*. NY: Guilford Press.

Evans, D., Jeckel, L., & Slott, N. (1982). Erotomania: A variant of pathological mourning. *Bulletin of the Menninger Clinic, 46*, 507-520.

Orion, D. (1997). *I know you really love me*. NY: Macmillan.

One Case, Many Conversations:
Toward Multiplicities

Mary Ballou
Gretchen Schmelzer

SUMMARY. The focus of this article is discussions about a complex life situation of a school-age inner-city African American girl seen for mental health services. The discussion reflects the points of view of a doctoral intern and a faculty member. A number of individual, developmental and sociocultural issues are addressed. Some attempt to relate contextual issues to therapeutic actions is undertaken. The article ends with some reflection on the shared process of discussion and article writing. *[Article copies available for a fee from The Haworth Document Delivery Service: 1-800-342-9678. E-mail address: getinfo@haworthpressinc.com]*

Therapeutic failure. It is not a topic commonly discussed or written about. This is an article about a case that felt like a therapeutic failure, and

---

This listing is alphabetical. The article is a collaborative effort.

Mary Ballou is Associate Professor of Counseling Psychology at Northeastern University. In addition to teaching and research, she practices counseling and therapy in both urban and rural settings. She also consults with nonprofit women's groups. Gretchen Schmelzer is a third year doctoral student in Counseling Psychology at Northeastern University. She comes to Counseling Psychology from active engagement in Sport Psychology, and currently works primarily with children, adolescents and families. This is her first professional publication.

Address correspondence to Mary Ballou, CRS, 203 Lake Hall, Northeastern University, Boston, MA 02115.

[Haworth co-indexing entry note]: "One Case, Many Conversations: Toward Multiplicities." Ballou, Mary and Gretchen Schmelzer. Co-published simultaneously in *Women & Therapy* (The Haworth Press, Inc.) Vol. 21, No. 3, 1998, pp. 13-29; and: *Learning from Our Mistakes: Difficulties and Failures in Feminist Therapy* (ed: Marcia Hill and Esther D. Rothblum) The Haworth Press, Inc., 1998, pp. 13-29. Single or multiple copies of this article are available for a fee from The Haworth Document Delivery Service [1-800-342-9678, 9:00 a.m. - 5:00 p.m. (EST). E-mail address: getinfo@haworthpressinc.com].

13

the many conversations it took to come to understand the work in this case. The reader will hear my (Gretchen's) voice as the therapist, Mary's voice as the structural analyst and senior therapist, and these voices together to give perspective to the client's struggle. Though still a student, I have a large library, and the term therapeutic failure is not listed in a single one of my books. The closest discussion is the "therapeutic impasse" (Bergman & Surrey, 1992; Jordan, 1989) or countertransference issues which interrupt or impede treatment (Pearlman & Saakvitne, 1995). In written Chinese, the word "crisis" is a combination of the symbols "opportunity" and "danger." The American Heritage Dictionary (1983) defines "crisis" as a crucial, or decisive point; a turning point. Perhaps the word "crisis" more accurately reflects the intensity of the therapeutic struggle than the word failure.

From the clinician's standpoint, a therapeutic crisis might be defined as the failure to be an adequate guide in the mutual struggle up the peak that the client must climb. The therapist might be unaware of, or unwilling to acknowledge, a whole range of climbing perils. Maybe her rope and equipment are not up to the task. Maybe her knowledge of climbing, or of this particular terrain, is shaky. Maybe she is simply too tired to complete the climb, or maybe she has misjudged the client, and the client is not ready to climb that particular mountain. Or from a broader perspective, perhaps a bigger climbing party was needed. Maybe the timing was wrong and it is too treacherous to climb now, or maybe the region's politics make climbing there unsafe.

The therapeutic relationship, like any good climb, entails ups and downs. There are places along the trail which afford clear perspectives to both the therapist and the client, and places where the going is rough. Sometimes the footholds and handholds are readily apparent; sometimes you can't see your way up. As a student-guide, I am very aware that I am often unsure of the next bit of terrain—wishing that I had a map, that the fog would thin, that there was a guide ahead of me.

This is a story about one therapeutic relationship, a school-year-long climb, where I encountered many such therapeutic crises or turning points. In this case there were numerous therapeutic moments of connection, healing and movement. Yet, this case came immediately to mind when the issue of "therapeutic failure" was raised. It was complex, and overall, my goal of creating a system of safety, both internal (coping skills) and external (school and communities resources) was not met. In metaphorical terms, I feel as though I left my client on that very dangerous mountain, guideless.

THE CONTEXT: CLIENT, THERAPIST, AND THERAPY

The Client

Liza is an 11 year old African American girl. She was initially referred to counseling by her maternal grandmother because she was not eating. In addition, Liza's classroom teachers were concerned because she was moody and sullen, and had poor peer interactions. Liza was a regular education student in the fifth grade.

Liza was not viewed positively in the classroom. She was seen as "not working up to her potential," as a "troublemaker who sets other children up" and as a hypochondriac. The school also had a negative view of this family. Liza's mother, Ms. A., and Liza's grandmother were perceived as coming to school only to "fight" on behalf of their children. The school personnel felt that they often ignored the school's other attempts to work with them. The school nurse felt that Liza often "complained about nothing."

Liza at 11 was the older of two children. Her brother was nine and attended the same elementary school. Ms. A. had Liza at the age of eighteen. Both children had different fathers, neither of whom was actively involved in the life of the family. Ms. A.'s husband recently died of AIDS. Ms. A. stated that she is also HIV positive, but is choosing not to tell her children. When treatment began, Ms. A. and her two children were living with her parents. According to Ms. A., there was a history of violence and substance use both in her family-of-origin and in her relationship with her recently deceased husband.

Liza's early years were spent living with mom who lived with various boyfriends or in the home of her maternal grandmother. Most recently, two years ago, when Ms. A.'s husband was very ill with AIDS, Ms. A. left her children in the care of her mother while she lived with him. The children only saw their mother sporadically; the couple was forced to live in a variety of motels and shelters during this time, and connected rarely with the children. Ms. A. returned to her children after his death. She was extremely depressed and was unable to focus on the needs of her children. She was struggling with grief over her companion's death, her own illness, housing issues, employment issues, and what appeared to be a significant trauma history. Over the course of the year Ms. A. moved herself and her two children to a homeless shelter and began the process of trying to find housing on her own.

Liza's principal coping strategy was to hunker down and conserve her limited internal resources. Typically she dealt with stress by withdrawing and sucking her thumb. She frequently refused to go to school, pleading illness. To continue the earlier metaphor, she would stop in her tracks and cling desperately to the side of the mountain, refusing to go up or down. To complicate matters, her body belied this "little girl" coping strategy; she had the physical build of a 17-year-old.

The Therapist

I (Gretchen) am a third year doctoral student in a counseling psychology program. I am female and Caucasian. I was a trainee for a child service agency that runs an outpatient counseling clinic within an inner city public school. As part of this training experience I received individual supervision from two supervisors and group supervision through my graduate program. The supervisors at the agency worked within a psychodynamic treatment model focusing on a developmental and relational understanding of a child's assessment and treatment. The university program's view was ecological. The ecological model conceptualizes or sees the individual in context, that is, it considers the structural forces upon the individual and holds in awareness multiple and varied social causative influences in an individual's difficulties.

My previous work experience has been primarily with adolescents in residential settings, so this was my first experience with community based outpatient mental health. Working in residential settings has given me a different set of assumptions about how to understand and create holding environments for clients. In a residential setting, the therapy hour is only one of twenty-four therapeutic hours–you learn to be very humble about your work in relation to all of the other healing which is occurring in that setting. This has made me especially aware that mine is but one of the other hours in a client's life, and not to put too much weight on the one that I can provide.

I also come to my work with six years of work in Sport Psychology. I am used to understanding individuals in context of group dynamics, both clients and those who work with them. Sports counseling is also focused on building on a client's strengths, and knowing that psychological skills, like an athlete's physical skills, require time and practice to be learned and applied.

The Therapy

I saw Liza individually, during the school day over the course of nine months. Therapy was supposed to occur weekly for forty-five minute sessions, though due to her absenteeism, our meetings were more sporadic. Liza was often shy and silent, and she would sometimes cover her mouth when she smiled. I could get a sense of how our interaction was going to be by whether she walked ahead of me, with me, or behind me on the way from her classroom to my office.

Early in the year we talked while playing board games. She enjoyed winning, but was very concerned if I lost by too much. In fact, she would often refuse to take my play money, or would give me half of her money if she felt I was too "poor." It seemed to me that it was important to Liza that I have "enough" to care for her. Although the initial concern was related to her eating, it became clear that Liza was having difficulty in many areas of her life: she was not attending school regularly, she was not completing her classwork, and she did not have good relationships with peers. The case, as I understood it, grew more complicated as she shared her interests in boys, and as her mother revealed their life circumstances. In addition, there was always a sense of starting from the beginning with Liza. Each session felt like a first session, so we were in a constant state of saying "hello." This dynamic of always saying hello seemed to serve a protective purpose for Liza, to test whether I would be consistent in my effort to interact with her. The "hellos" formed a ritual to help her control the pace of the relationship. It was my assumption that her previous experience in relationships did not include safety or trust, and she had developed this style of interacting as a way of managing relational closeness which she felt overwhelmed by.

Initially, the goals in this case were to assess eating, and to try to intervene in her school and relational functioning. As I grew more concerned about her emotional and physical safety, I shifted the goals in my mind to make her safety my primary focus. My concerns about her safety centered on her relationships with boys, her uncertain living circumstances, all exacerbated by her poor coping skills and her inability to connect to others who could help. Most of all, I wanted to be able to assure her safety in the future by connecting her to future school resources.

In a session occurring during a family crisis (an aunt had been stabbed by an ex-boyfriend), Liza began to discuss phone calls with boys. These conversations grew to become her primary focus during our time together. Therapy ended with the completion of the school year, both because Liza was graduating to a new school, and because I was ending my practicum placement.

THE CLIMB: DANGER AND OPPORTUNITY

This case presented many crisis points in the sense of turning points or intervention points. The first crisis in this case for me was to figure out which trail to take up the mountain. What is the therapeutic frame for this case? Who is the client? What should individual therapy look like in a case like this? Where should I begin? What should my priority be? I conceptualized this case within an ecological framework, and was supervised individually within a psychodynamic perspective. I struggled with a sense of hopelessness about where to intervene in this complex case. There were many crises to pay attention to. In response, I chose to first pay attention to the systems in which Liza was developing, home and school, to understand her dilemma better. The mother had few resources with which to parent, though she clearly loved her children. She was HIV positive which made me concerned about the children's future. Who would care for the children when the mother's health declined? This uncertainty about the mother's future seemed to drive me towards wanting to assure some sort of future planning or safety for Liza. While the grandmother would probably step in, that household was not described as a safe haven for the children. The grandfather was alcoholic, there were various uncles and family members living in the home at any given time, and the supervision of the children was unclear.

Liza's most basic needs, food and housing, were presenting concerns. They were living either in the living room of the grandmother's house or in a shelter, so getting services for the family was difficult because they were always on the verge of moving. Ms. A. was trying to finish her GED, but she was extremely depressed and slept much of the time.

Liza came to school sporadically, and was always behind on her work. The teachers were reluctant to hold her accountable for her missed work, not wanting to punish her. Therefore, it was difficult to begin to make a case to get extra services when she was a regular education student in "good" standing. When the school finally filed against the family for truancy, I was hopeful that she would be eligible for a caseworker or truancy officer who could join the team and be a resource for Liza. As it turns out, truancy carries very little weight; they simply give the offender a warning, so that particular path led nowhere.

Liza was not the classic resilient child (Brooks, 1994), that is, the child who despite difficult odds has the outgoing temperament to connect to adults or peers and get her needs met. In fact, Liza was disliked by most adults and peers. She had many somatic complaints. These somatic complaints appeared to be Liza's way of showing that she hurt. She also seemed to protect herself from rejection by not allowing others to get too close.

Despite the many presented and interpreted clinical issues, the main therapeutic crisis discussed in this paper revolves around sex. The first discussion Liza and I had about boys and sex began with her telling me that she couldn't wait to go home and call "friends." After dropping these hints she became very quiet, essentially withdrawing from the conversation. In an attempt to elicit information I began a style of interacting which matched her hint-dropping pattern, and it became a question and answer game. For example, I might ask "which friends?," or "a boy or girl?" I gained little information from this game initially, but Liza appeared to enjoy the attention it provided. I noticed that the conversation had an adolescent feel to it. And I imagined that it may have been similar in question/answer to the conversations she was having with the boys.

Over the course of our sessions together, Liza described spending many hours on the phone. She talked about a boyfriend. She said that other boys were calling her, too, and that one of them wanted a "birthday present" from her and that she wasn't going to give it to him, though she had given these "presents" before. She smiled and looked down–once again, an invitation to play our question/answer game. I asked her what the present was. She said that she couldn't say. I asked whether it was something she bought or something she did. She said that it was something she did. I asked if it were a kiss. She said it was like a kiss, but wasn't going to talk any more about it.

I was confused about how to understand the problem and where to intervene. I was staring at an eleven-year-old who was sucking her thumb; yet I had the sense we were having a conversation about oral sex. I did not want to be judgmental, because I wanted her to be able to talk to me. I was searching in my mind for a right answer, a therapeutic must in this situation. I alternately wanted to rescue her and hoped someone would rescue me. I explored whether she could talk to her mother about sex and boys (in other words, is someone *else* in your life handling this more adequately than I am?). I asked whether she knew about pregnancy and AIDS. However, I failed to explore what she actually knew.

At the end of the session I walked Liza back to her classroom, and went back to my office to write up my case notes. I knew I felt stuck, but wasn't sure where. This case had felt complex before, but now it felt desperate. I began to doubt my interaction with her and how I had handled this conversation about sex. There were many competing needs to balance in this conversation. The complications and dangers of sexuality for an eleven-year-old compelled action, yet the lack of trust and closeness in the relationship seemed to disallow such action. Direct conversation felt intrusive, and thus the question/answer format seemed to be the clearest path. Should I have changed the interaction, and if so, to what?

My problem wasn't how to convey information about sexual matters, per se; it was how to have a conversation that carried so much affective weight for both of us. I can recall discussing this case in every supervision opportunity I had. I would relate my concerns about Liza's sexual activity and yet barely raised my difficulty in addressing it. I felt, perhaps, that at this point in my career/education I *shouldn't* be having difficulty with these conversations. The parallel process was striking: perhaps, I too, was hoping for some sort of question and answer game. This is where crisis became an opportunity. I used this opportunity to seek out and use a variety of resources to understand Liza and my interaction with her. I talked to supervisors, classmates, and professors about their complex cases. In these conversations I learned a lot about the limits of the role of an individual therapist. Supervisors discussed their difficult cases and shared their frustration about what could and could not occur with an individual therapy context. Classmates also were willing to share their frustrations as well as suggestions for options that worked for them within the public school or social service arenas. I also used my own resources, therapeutic and spiritual, to help me pay attention to my interaction in this case. Like many others in the helping professions, I struggle with needing to feel like I can "fix" something–and this case seemed to stir up more of my "fix it" feelings than the others. I found that it was important for me to pay attention to when I was responding to an internal drive to "fix it," rather than staying present and responding to Liza's actual needs in the relationship.

The second major conversation about sex revolved around her relationship with one older boy. I never got the actual age but this was clearly someone very important to Liza. This was, however, a very different conversation from the first. Though the conversation still had the question and answer feel to it, I added a new component, where I would narrate how the game was connecting us in conversation. I was able to help her notice the way our question and answer game kept us both connected and disconnected during our conversation. I'm still not sure whether this approach helped her, and whether this was a better way to have such a conversation, but I felt better about making our game an overt conversation. I felt good about this interaction, but the fears around a sexually active eleven-year-old left me still feeling that in some way I was not addressing her safety needs around sexuality.

THE VIEW: A STRUCTURAL ANALYSIS

A structural analysis of selected clinical points raised in Liza's case will, Mary believes, add an important dimension to Gretchen's climb. As therapists working with clients, and as educators working with prospective therapists, we have generally been insufficiently aware of the contextual or surrounding extra-psychological factors. These include fundamental structural, systemic, and institutional factors. In particular, what has been lacking is an awareness of how these factors influence the lives of our clients and our clinical thinking and work. Clear understanding of structural, systemic and institutional factors requires analyses aimed at historical and contemporary views of economic, political and social arenas. These perspectives are generally kept quite separate from the training and professional journals of mental health disciplines. Yet merely economic, political and social perspectives are not adequate for mental health work either, because they leave out substantial consideration of the subtle and obvious influences on multiple dimensions of human development over the life span. The tensions and multiplicities of interdisciplinary views offer direction for understanding the personal human impact(s) of socially controlling political and economic forces.

One significant structural view is furnished through consideration of the distribution of wealth and resources in contemporary U.S. society. Clearly, neither Liza's family nor the social systems with which she interacts can offer her the resources required to assure her a safe and nurturing environment. Scarce resource models are being applied to human safety and security needs in our current market economy. Social programs funded by the government are no longer readily available. Secure housing, food and safe environments were simply not part of Liza's formative experience. So far, the damages she sustained and her response to them were not visible enough to draw the attention and intervention of the over-burdened social services. In major cities, and increasingly in smaller cities and towns, state agencies and their agents–mandated reporters, shackled by the lack of resources, staff, and funds–are choosing/forced to disregard truancy, withdrawn behavior, premature sexual activities, and even suspicions of abuse. Despite the economic, safety and security difficulties and their psychological and behavioral sequelae, the current scarce resource model for human needs means even worse damage must occur before assistance is made available to Liza. This case gives us a glimpse of the realities of poverty in the lived experience of an urban African American girl. In conventional psychological terms we might label this a chaotic family; in feminist terms we would call it multiple oppressions. Either view should extend its analysis to the impacts of welfare policy reform and its accompanying budget cuts, that is, redistribution of resources from need to greed.

Assisting Liza is a major dilemma for any therapist. Conventional psychotherapy does not contain the scope of roles necessary to assist Liza. Clearly social-cultural engineering is needed. Although replete with developmental needs in psychological, cognitive, educational and relational terms, the case is far too complicated by sociopolitical and structural factors to be satisfactorily conceptualized or contained within psychotherapy frameworks. Even to establish a revised goal of safety for Liza, as was done in this case, was not possible given the lack of socio-structural resources. The most adequate response offered in human services is case management, since we often think of case management as providing models for action in similar cases.

Therapist interns are not typically trained to do case management. If they did know how and it were defined within their helping roles, they would have no authority to access those resources. Finally, however, case work is a concept of social services carried over from decades past, when social policy directed itself to the needs of all citizens. In the current political climate, there are not enough resources available within schools and communities to address the needs. The emphasis for case manager has become more of state agent. In concert with conservative public ideology and drastically reduced public assistance funds, case management on behalf of our clients is endangered. Agency policies, huge case loads and thoroughly inadequate resources in every area lead to its redefinition. It is frequently used as an arm of the state law enforcement investigating for abuse, placement, and custody, instead of a supportive resource for assisting with the needs of individuals and families. In the present discussion, neither Gretchen nor the school could expect responses to Liza's needs through state assistance. While Gretchen kept faith to Liza's needs, the school seems to reduce its view to individual culpability.

Liza's case is multifaceted and it includes the complexities of multiply nondominant groups. It offers an appropriate context from which we can scrutinize the adequacy of conventional psychology for providing human service. Race-ethnic, class and gender normative standards are highly relevant considerations in the establishment of treatment goals or therapeutic aims. The dominant normative criteria foundational in conventional theories of psychotherapy are upper-middle class, EuroAmerican and masculine. Yet the life experience fitting to these criteria is not the life experience of Liza. Coping skills and peer relationships are two of the clinical issues in Liza's case. Liza's survival within her cultural context required that she identify with and be accepted by the inner city African American community, and that she secure her place within a network of kinship. The interpersonal skills she needs to develop in order to meet these survival and safety requirements are not likely to include conventional dominant culture social skills. Instead her coping and relational survival skills included strategic withdrawal and bartering with neighborhood males for protection/affection in exchange for sexualized attention. Standards for 'normal,' 'adaptive,' 'healthy' behavior are not universal, as most conventional psychotherapy holds. Rather most co-cultures and nondominant groups have their own norms and norms that vary within group and change over time.

Gretchen's refocusing from eating disorders and school performance to increasing awareness of safety needs through coping skills and accessing school and community resources in Liza's own contextual terms is an important understanding. Though these could not be achieved, through psychotherapy and insufficient resources, the needs were correctly identified.

In a somewhat similar yet expanded structural view, imperialism and colonial rule are additional considerations to Liza's case. Imperialism is a term that has global historic and economic origins. Its recent use within psychology has not been generally associated with the militaristic and expansionistic actions of colonial domination in the 18th and 19th centuries (Leahey, 1993). Yet the essential meaning of imperialism, impositions of worldviews, customs, and traditions of the dominant group on less powerful group in such a way as to obliterate, cover over or subvert the functioning, values, and beliefs of the nondominant group, is an important consideration (Brown & Ballou, 1992; Harding, 1993; Said, 1994; Sanchez & Garriga, 1996).

From an imperialistic perspective, to see Liza as appropriately served by dominant group norms and then to pathologize her distance from them is to colonize her. To be unaware that criteria are relative and instead hold dominant group norms as universal is no longer tolerable. It is unacceptable because ignorance or merely changing surface language benefits the dominant group. For underneath a lack of awareness or insensitivity is intentionality and accruing of privilege. Understanding imperialism is useful because it connects conditions of power, resources, and status to discussions of racism, classism, and sexism. In the case at hand, conventional psychopathology, whether informed by individualistic psychodynamic or learning views or by family system views, reflects both the imperialism of Western psychology and a colonization of Liza. Naming Liza's problem as an eating disorder or poor attachment or her family as chaotic, would have masked the psychosocial consequences of classism, sexism and racism. Gretchen did well to escape imperialistic views within the diagnostic thinking, instead establishing creation of safety as an outcome goal.

FROM PANORAMA TO PARTICULARS:
APPLICATIONS OF THE STRUCTURAL ANALYSIS

A structural analysis naturally broadens the view, from the trail to the mountain range. Holding broader views with multiple perspectives of contexts is proving to be essential to contemporary viewpoints of human functioning and factors of influence. However, in doing psychotherapy, one must necessarily go back to the view of the trail ahead. The question is, how does understanding the view inform the choices the therapist will make along the way? Interdisciplinary perspectives that examine the external factors and also attend to the personal and interpersonal are not yet well developed in psychotherapy. A competent and ethical therapist is constantly engaged in the process of watching the particulars in relation to the context. The structural analysis is a way of expanding the context. Sauzier (1997) suggests integrating multiple perspectives as a way of intervening from context to therapy. This is illustrated well in Sauzier's recent article that discusses this process in doing play therapy and shifting to trauma assessment.

For instance, the most notable constant raised by the structural analysis in Liza's case was the striking lack of resources. All players, individual and institutional, in this case lacked the necessary resources to move this young girl towards a place of safety. Ms. A. lacked her own internal resources, both emotional and physical. She lacked familial and financial support. She was without housing or employment. Gretchen, as Liza's therapist, had a relative lack of experience, and difficulty having the necessary conversations in therapy and in supervision to communicate effectively. The institutions withheld their limited resources because Liza did not fit their profile of a child in crisis. For example, the school did not place Liza in a special classroom, because her "problem behavior" did not disturb others. Similarly, the legal system did not see truancy, a passive problem, to require resources or attention. Social services would not respond because Ms. A. had already moved her children out of an unsafe home. Not surprisingly, Liza was a child with few internal or external resources.

So if the structural analysis helped to clarify the problem as one of resources, how would it lead a therapist to act? What good is the broader view? As we discussed this case, it became clear that the therapeutic answer to the problem was not in *providing* resources, but in openly acknowledging their absence. What was missing from the interventions with Liza and Ms. A. were some very difficult conversations about limited resources. To have had such therapy conversations about the context of their lives might have served to name, to clarify, to understand, and to also externalize and thus to lay the ground for their own empowering. It is interesting to note that conversation about sex became the initial flashpoint, perhaps because conversations about sex are difficult. However, there were many more difficult conversations to have. To talk about scarce resources, whether internal, familial, political or institutional is to bring some very sad and angry truths to light. Not to discuss them is to disallow the client a chance to narrate her story and also withhold understanding her story in its class (poverty), gender (sexism) and racial-ethnic (racism)–sociocultural–contexts.

For Liza and her mother these conversations would have taken many forms. Had Gretchen's conversations with Ms. A. been more concrete and clear about Liza's needs and the limits of what she as a mother could provide, it may have allowed a greater opportunity to resource problem solve, to help her parent, and for Liza. Also had Liza been included in these resource and parenting discussions, she could have benefited from listening to the adults problem solve and discuss her welfare.

Conversations in therapy with Liza could have included more discussions of her struggles in terms of resources, especially in relation to poverty, and living with a mom who was under stress. Initially, Gretchen balked at this idea as we discussed it, thinking that abstract conversations about resources would be too difficult for an eleven-year-old. However, we came to see that conversation can take many forms. Metaphors and stories can go a long way in communicating these ideas, in addition to some straight conversations about facts.

Multiple perspectives are brought together in the issue of meaning making. For a therapist, what does it mean to intervene in Liza's case? The fact of the matter is that therapy is intended and organized to help people function better in their lives. This ultimately translates to mental health in the service of maintaining the status quo. The challenge then, is to help clients articulate their struggles and make meaning of them in such a way as to see and act for change, both individual and social. In Liza's case, this might have meant helping Ms. A. engage other resources, such as challenging the school, social systems or her own community(s) to provide more services. Or perhaps this might have meant getting Liza to challenge her mother to provide more structure or resources in terms of parenting.

Lastly, the issue of meaning making and hard conversation should include conversations about the therapy itself. Being willing to discuss the meaning and limits of the therapeutic relationship is an opportunity to model the kind of conversation this case required. What did it mean to Liza and her mother to have a counselor in their life? Perhaps voicing the quandary of wanting to get Liza to attend school and not having the power to make it happen, would have allowed Liza and Gretchen to negotiate the limits and value of therapy. Often the therapist's desire to fix the problems also serves to protect from the sense of powerlessness that we cannot. So involved, the opportunity to see what actually could be done is often lost.

Conversations about the therapy relationship also allow for communication about what is needed at any given time. DeChillo, Koren and Schultze (1994) interviewed families about their experience in therapy. They found that though the "partnership" of a therapeutic relationship was often viewed as a 50-50 split, families often wanted either the therapist to take more of a lead, or less of a lead. Therapy relationships are not a constant 50-50 split, but instead, a dynamic and fluid entity. Open dialogue is the only method to ascertain such information.

To model exploration of resources, supervisors might help trainees by having similarly context based conversations. For example, discussing the limits and resources of supervision for the trainee or the case would illustrate how supervision is affected by the contextual factors and actions resultant from them. Hard conversations, many conversations, through multiple perspectives provide opportunity to explore context and meaning as a way to move from panorama to particular interventions.

REFLECTIONS: THE SPACE BETWEEN

In this ending Mary and Gretchen reflect upon the experiences together. A description of a process rarely does the process justice–it is a little like trying to describe what a quickly moving river looks like. The description of this case and the crisis within it, and the structural analysis are only one part of the learning from this experience. For us, the striking part of this experience came from our interaction: this experience was made up of constant dialogue. Right from the beginning, there was dialogue: which case to discuss, concerns about client confidentiality and what constituted a "failure," what was worth examining.

This dialogue was not without its hitches–we come from different backgrounds, have different levels of experience, and different points of view. Yet, once settled on a case, we began to create a space for the discussion of Liza, Gretchen's interaction with her, and Mary's understanding of the two. It seems that it was this "work space" which allowed for a different type of conversation about the work of therapy. This "space between," as Grunebaum (1990) refers to it, is a place where such dialogue can occur. There is much to learn from this experience in this space about traditional supervision practices and the process of reflecting on a case.

For me, Mary, the space between was a delicate balance between roles, activities, perspectives and developmental stages. It was a busy place filled with choices guided through the changing present dynamics between us. My goal was to participate with Gretchen as she began the act of writing about her reflections on her clinical work. Now instead of talking to clients, she was to begin talking with colleagues. My time was busy supporting, figuring, encouraging and teaching. Yet the activities felt more akin to baking together than to class or consulting room teaching. Much as in the process of baking, we talked about what we would make, who might eat it, and how much to make. We discussed procedures, the use of substitute resources, and which of us would do which part, as well as about budgets and nutritional values. Finally, as in a collaborative baking effort, we laughed, joked, and had fun. Yet there was also the awareness that I was more experienced and held a responsibility carrying role. With this sense of responsibility came the awareness that our life experiences, relative status positions, and developmental stages led to different points of view. While my effort was to the creation of this project, my obligation was also to Gretchen's baking skills, and to the pleasure and nutritional needs of those she might feed in the future.

For me, Gretchen, the process that Mary and I went through was not unlike supervision in some respects. She is a senior therapist; I brought in struggles and looked to her to gain some clarity. However, unlike an actual supervisory relationship, fraught with dual relationships and conflicts of interest, Mary was neither responsible for the actual welfare of my client, nor was she responsible for my evaluation as a therapist. We also had the luxury of time, both because the case was over, and there was no pressure to actually intervene, and because we could continue our discussions as long as we wanted–and not have to move onto another case, or another meeting, as is reality in the actual supervision of an intern's cases.

This "space between" was not created by us through an initial verbal negotiation. Much like the work with our clients (and our supervisors), the negotiations of roles, goals, and content evolve over time through dialogue(s) and action(s). Our space was negotiated with each question and "wondering aloud" about the case. I noticed that the space was affected by my ability to know "where I was." That is, when I tried to follow Mary too closely, agreed prematurely, or assumed I understood a concept, I closed up the space. When I held back and wasn't sure whether to bring information into the space, it left Mary without something to engage.

Yet, this space is not just about "relationality," that is, our ability to be present or authentic in conversation. It was also about the willingness to explore this case from many different levels–to bring some "space" into our understanding of our work and really look at the impact these multiple views have on a case, and how these perspectives interact with each other. For example, the "space" was opened to look at developmental issues not only for Liza, but how they interacted with my development as a therapist. It was opened to look at structural forces affecting Liza's family, affecting my ability to discuss the case in supervision, and our ability to discuss the case for this article. All aspects of the case, all the participants in the dialogue were viewed from as many different angles as possible. For example, how did an imperialist understanding of Liza allow us to understand my interventions, and other possible interventions?

This process was exciting because it allowed a freedom of understanding Liza and my frustration with the case far from the "individual blaming" (either Liza or myself) which is so prevalent. But it was also maddening. Continually expanding perspectives of a client's world becomes too vast and difficult to take in. How do you gain the ability to pull back and see the whole mountain range, and yet know where to put your next footfall? I often balked at the larger frame–wanting to close up some of the "space between." I found myself wanting to find my one mistake, the one thing that I could fix, so that future cases could go smoothly. Mary, however, was persistent. She would come from the other direction and asked if I'd looked at this, or at that. She was willing to look at the whole view.

For a therapist to look at the whole picture, to sit and stare at the whole view, is to sit in awe. It is this awe, this respect for our client's life circumstances and struggles, and for our own learning, which brings the compassion and humanity to our work.

REFERENCES

Bergman, S., & Surrey, J. (1992). The woman-man relationship: Impasses and possibilities. Work in Progress, No. 55. Wellesley, MA: Stone Center Working Paper Series.

Brooks, R. (1994). Children at risk: Fostering resilience and hope. *American Journal of Orthopsychiatry, 64*, 545-553.

Brown, L., & Ballou, M. (Eds.). (1992). *Personality and psychopathology: Feminist reappraisals*. New York: Guilford.

DeChillo, N., Koren, P., & Schultze, K. (1994). From paternalism to partnership: Family and professional collaboration in children's mental health. *American Journal of Orthopsychiatry, 64*, 564-576.

Grunebaum, J. (1990). From discourse to dialogue: The power of fairness in therapy with couples. In R. Chasin, H. Grunebaum, & M. Herzig (Eds.), *One Couple, Four Realities* (pp. 191-228). New York: Guilford.

Harding, S. (Ed.). (1993). *The racial economy of science*. Bloomington: Indiana University Press.

Jordan, J. (1989). Relational development: Therapist implications of empathy and shame. Work in Progress, No. 39. Wellesley, MA: Stone Center Working Paper Series.

Leahey, T. (1993). *A history of psychology: Main currents in psychological thought.* Englewood Cliffs, NJ: Prentice Hall.

Pearlman, L., & Saakvitne, K. (1995). *Trauma and the Therapist.* New York: W.W. Norton.

Said, E. (1994). *Culture and imperialism.* New York: Vantage Books.

Sanchez, W., & Garriga, O. (1996). Psychotherapy, Puerto Ricans and Colonialism: The Issue of Awareness. *Latino Studies Journal 7* (2), 29-50.

Sauzier, M. (1997). Memories of trauma in the treatment of children. In P. Appelbaum, L. Uyehara, & M. Elin (Eds.). *Trauma and memory: Clinical and legal controversies* (pp. 378-393). New York: Oxford.

Self-Disclosure as an Approach to Teaching Ethical Decision-Making

Ellen Cole

SUMMARY. The author examines a difficult case that confronted her with a variety of ethical issues: individual therapy within the context of couples' therapy, problems encountered by rural therapists, and the question of when to refer. She presented this case to graduate counseling students to analyze and critique. The students recognized, as a result of this activity, that real-life ethical dilemmas are more complex than textbook examples, that there is a difference between aspirational principles and absolute standards, and that the ethical decision-making process is key. When an instructor presents her own imperfect work, she encourages students to be open about their real concerns. *[Article copies available for a fee from The Haworth Document Delivery Service: 1-800-342-9678. E-mail address: getinfo@haworthpressinc.com]*

I have two purposes in writing this article. The first is to explore what for me was a difficult therapy case; the second is to suggest the use of

---

Ellen Cole, PhD, directs the Master of Science in Counseling Psychology program at Alaska Pacific University in Anchorage and co-chairs the Alaska Psychological Association Ethics Committee. Certified as a sex therapist by the American Association of Sex Educators, Counselors, and Therapists, she has practiced sex therapy since 1975. She has edited and authored numerous publications about sexuality and women's mental health.

The author would like to thank her colleagues, Cleary Donovan and Robert A. Lane, and her graduate students, particularly Laura M. Brooks, Greta L. Eidem, and Jackie Warren, for their comments on this article.

[Haworth co-indexing entry note]: "Self-Disclosure as an Approach to Teaching Ethical Decision-Making." Cole, Ellen. Co-published simultaneously in *Women & Therapy* (The Haworth Press, Inc.) Vol. 21, No. 3, 1998, pp. 31-39; and: *Learning from Our Mistakes: Difficulties and Failures in Feminist Therapy* (ed: Marcia Hill and Esther D. Rothblum) The Haworth Press, Inc., 1998, pp. 31-39. Single or multiple copies of this article are available for a fee from The Haworth Document Delivery Service [1-800-342-9678, 9:00 a.m. - 5:00 p.m. (EST). E-mail address: getinfo@haworthpressinc.com].

actual cases (heavily disguised, of course), particularly ones that feel unresolved, in teaching ethical decision-making to graduate students who are pursuing careers as psychotherapists. The use of actual cases, I believe, serves to demonstrate "the slippery slope" of ethical decision-making (Pope, Sonne, & Holroyd, 1994) as well as the uncertainty experienced even by long-time therapists like myself. I believe that to the extent that we can be fallible and real human beings with our students, they in turn will share with us and with their clinical supervisors their real concerns. This in turn will produce therapists of the future who will be able to know themselves well, monitor their own behavior adequately, and turn to others for consultation without shame. Our clients of course are the ultimate beneficiaries.

Such is a case I brought to class a few weeks ago. Although it's a case from 15 years ago, and one with a happy ending, it has pulled at the back of my conscience all these years as a case I may have bungled and certainly did not adequately understand. I made an effort, both with my students and now in this article, to present myself as a therpist who felt buffeted during the course of this case between conflicting needs and responsibilities.

I begin this article with the brief case description, interspersed with questions, that I handed out in class, and the students' initial response. I chose this particular case because it represents a number of ethical dilemmas: an issue common to couples therapy, the appropriateness of seeing one of the couple individually; the special problems of the rural or small community therapist; and the question of referral.

CASE DESCRIPTION

Celeste, an attorney, and Robert, a fishing guide, were referred to me for sex therapy by Celeste's gynecologist. They had been married for 12 years and had three school-age children. The presenting problem from Celeste's point of view was that Robert did not like sex. From his perspective, Celeste was "oversexed" and "wanted it all the time." Each wanted therapy, each wanted their sexual relationship to change.

I saw them together for an initial consultation session and took individual histories the following week. I concluded that Robert, who considered himself underemployed, suffered from previously undiagnosed mild but lifelong depression. I suggested he see a psychiatrist for a depression screening, but he refused (this was a time when a diagnosis of depression was much less acceptable to clients than it is today). Celeste, on the other hand, was enjoying both her flourishing career and the fact that her children were now in school all day. She'd dedicated her adult life to being a "good woman," balancing career and family, and described herself as "a blossoming flower." While emotionally in very different places, Celeste and Robert nevertheless seemed committed to each other and to their family unity. I proceeded to design a sex therapy treatment plan consisting of weekly office psychotherapy combined with touching and communication exercises for them to do at home.

I saw Celeste and Robert for four more sessions, and they seemed to be doing well. At that point, Celeste called and asked for an individual appointment. She declined, on the phone, to tell me what she wanted to talk about. I asked if Robert knew she was calling me, and she said, "No." *[What should I have said to her? On what grounds?]*

Celeste and I met without Robert, and she told me that she had just begun a flirtatious relationship with a married man. They hadn't slept together yet, but she sensed it wouldn't be long. *[What do I say/do? Do I continue to work with her?]*

I encouraged her to go slowly, recommended a book about infidelity (these days my book of choice would be Frank Pittman's *Private Lies*, 1989), and gave my standard "don't do it, but if you do, make sure you use protection" talk. We discussed the pros and cons of her disclosing all this to Robert, and made an appointment (without Robert) for next week. *[What do I do about Robert at this point? Was it wrong to see Celeste alone after beginning couples' therapy?]*

Celeste came in the following week to tell me that she had "confessed" everything to Robert, they had consequently agreed to a separation, and she was indeed now having sex with the married man. She said, "I can't tell you his name, because you know him." At that point I immediately, intuitively, knew who the man was. I'll call him Mike. Mike was a movie-star-handsome man whom I had long suspected of having multiple, brief affairs, despite the fact that he and his wife, Johanna, had five children, including a newborn baby. Mike, Johanna, and my brother worked together; my brother, in fact, was Mike's direct supervisor in a local business. Celeste had also occasionally worked, as a contract attorney, for the same company. Mike, Johanna, my husband, and I had socialized together on numerous occasions at various town functions, and I considered Johanna to be a friend. *[What do I think/say/do?]*

THE REST OF THE STORY

My graduate students were very clear, immediately, in their response to this case. "You should not have seen Celeste alone after beginning couples' therapy. That was your first mistake. But as soon as you confirmed

Mike's identity (which I did as soon as I guessed it), it was entirely unethical for you to continue to see Celeste."

I responded by sharing with my students what actually occurred, along with my reflections at the time these events transpired, and some of my current understandings. The ensuing discussion took an hour and could have taken even longer if we had had the time. Here's what I shared with them.

When I initially agreed to see Celeste alone, I did not know what she was going to tell me. I asked her on the phone, but she wanted to wait until we were face-to-face. Even now, 15 years later, I sometimes suggest individual appointments for my sex therapy clients, always in the service of their development as a couple. (For instance, if an individual is having a strongly aversive reaction to the homework assignments, I might want to work one-on-one to reassess the appropriateness of sex therapy and possibly do some preparatory counseling.) At the time the individual appointment is set, some couples' therapists might say, "Yes, I can see you without your partner, but everything we talk about needs to be shared with her/him," while other therapists would not insist on disclosure. Without knowing the nature of what Celeste wanted to discuss, I did not establish any guidelines. Today I think I would adhere to what seems to be the predominant wisdom: no secrets if you want to continue to work with me. On the other hand, I might not say this on the telephone, for fear that a client would terminate therapy precipitously.

When Celeste first revealed her "flirtatious relationship" to me, I believe my responses were, even retrospectively, responsible and helpful. However, I still saw myself as doing couples' therapy, and I was uncomfortable and unsure about how to handle the fact that I knew something Robert did not know–something of great import to this couple. Therefore, I was relieved when Celeste made the decision to tell him everything.

Once Robert and Celeste separated, and Celeste began her active affair with the married man, she became extremely anxious, describing herself as "feeling out of control." She said she'd like to continue our individual meetings. I explored the possibility of her seeing a different therapist, even trying to convince her to do so. Not surprisingly, however, Celeste was adamant about wanting to continue to work with me. She argued that I knew her history; I was the only trained and certified sex therapist within hundreds of miles, and she wanted to explore sexual issues in therapy; nearly every other female therapist in this rural area had sought Celeste's legal services at one time or another (a male therapist was not a consideration for her); and although she didn't have the language to verbalize this, we had established a therapeutic bond.

With Celeste's consent, I phoned Robert and suggested an individual termination session to assess his well-being. He agreed readily to the appointment, at the end of which he said he would take my advice and begin his own individual work with a local male therapist.

Although one could argue, as my students did, that "once couples therapy, always couples therapy," and that I ought to have referred Celeste once the rules of the game changed, I decided to continue to see her for a variety of reasons which I will refer to throughout the remainder of this article. Understand, however, that as I continued to decide not to insist on a referral, I also continued to question the correctness of this decision–and continue to do so today.

At what point might I/should I have suggested, encouraged, or insisted upon a referral? When Celeste asked for an individual appointment? When she informed me she was flirting with someone? When she began to sleep with him? When I guessed his identity and realized there were multi-level entanglements that involved me, my brother, Celeste's lover, and Celeste's lover's wife? Might Celeste have perceived me as abandoning her at her time of greatest need, even perhaps punishing her for leaving her husband or having an affair with a married man? To whom could I have referred her, anyway? And would she have continued on with a different therapist? Was there a way I could continue to work with her? Did I want to? I was a member of a four-person peer supervision group at the time (two psychiatrists and two psychologists), and I put this case on the agenda for the following week.

My group was kind and supportive, perhaps too much so. I explained the situation, and they asked what I wanted to do. I answered, "I'd like to continue to work with Celeste. I think I can be helpful to her, and of course, as always, I will maintain strict silence at home." They advised me to tactfully bow out of social contacts with Mike and his family, wished me luck, and asked to be kept posted.

With time I've learned that peer supervision is difficult in two ways: (1) how I present to the group tends to shape their response and (2) by its nature members of a peer supervision group hold each other in high esteem, and, therefore, incline toward giving one another the benefit of the doubt. As one colleague put it, "I suspect that most of us carefully choose our words in such situations where we feel compelled to give criticism as we care about our peers and our relationship with them." This doesn't mean that peer supervision is not valuable; it means that ultimately we have to monitor ourselves, know ourselves well, engage in one-on-one consultation or psychotherapy when appropriate, and then do the best we can.

Within the following month there were two dramatic developments.

First, Celeste and Mike were "caught" by Johanna, who made the affair sensationally public by putting up Wanted posters in the Town Hall and the local General Store that included a photograph of Celeste and Mike in a compromising position. Second, Johanna phoned to tell me that she knew I was Celeste's therapist, and she thought I was a heel and a thoroughly rotten person for betraying her. She no longer considered me a friend and wanted never to see me again for as long as she lived.

LOOKING BACK

As I look back on this case from the perspective of many intervening years, I experience a variety of feelings and thoughts. First, I believe I did betray Johanna by continuing to work with Celeste after I knew of her affair with Mike. I made the decision to keep my client and not keep my friend, and my heart still hurts about that. At the same time, ending a therapeutic relationship because of loyalty to a friend could also be considered to be abandonment of my client.

Second, and this is the major issue, I ask myself why I felt compelled to continue to work with Celeste. A referral would have been difficult but not totally impossible.

I did not want to abandon her. Celeste and I had established a therapeutic bond. There was no point in time that seemed like the right time to refer (the slippery slope). We lived in a small town, and the other therapists, by dint of their gender or their business dealings with Celeste, were inappropriate. I was the only sex therapist in the area. She liked me; I liked her–and, at the risk of sounding defensive, this felt like more than a narcissistic "I am the only one." It felt like a true caring, a true desire to help, a familiar and laudable, perhaps even necessary, response to those with whom we work. And I believed it was the therapy that allowed her, while in the midst of a very unstable period of life, to maintain her work-life and continue to care for her children.

And what else was going on? On a deeper level, I enjoyed my hour each week with Celeste. I felt competent and admired. We laughed a lot and did good work together. That's what was in it for me. Deeper yet, and here we begin to enter the kind of territory that I believe exists for all therapists, if only we'd be willing to acknowledge and examine it, I believe I *had* convinced myself that I was the only one who could help her. (I now recognize this feeling as a red flag, a strong indication that this is more about me than my client, a reason for deep introspection and more than rubber-stamping consultation.) I believe that unadulterated curiosity was a factor, too. Maybe even voyeurism. A gorgeous woman and a movie-star guy were getting it on, and I got to hear about it. This was drama. I am drawn to emotional intensity, and here it was. (Even as I write these sentences I have to remind myself that these are common kinds of thoughts, that we therapists are humans, first, and this is why we get supervision.)

I believe I also wanted, although not consciously, to get the goods on Mike, even if there wasn't a thing in the world I could do about it. I didn't like what he did to his wife or to my client, and I believe in hindsight that I wanted to confirm my long-held suspicions about his philandering and deceit. I wanted to know, if only within myself, just how bad an apple he was.

The ultimate question was this: Did my overlapping relationships make it impossible for me to maintain a therapeutic stance? One answer is yes. Proof is that I still feel uncomfortable about this case after 15 years. But another answer is no. Proof is that Celeste progressed in therapy. She began as a woman who vacillated between the adolescent craving of immediate gratification and the self-sacrifice of a martyr. She ended with a much more balanced and intentional life. Maybe, as one of my students suspects, I just got lucky.

After a two-month fling with Mike, Celeste decided that if Robert would take her back, that's where she wanted to be. I saw them together three times and helped them work out specific guidelines for reunification. Celeste wanted Robert to continue his individual therapy to address his long-term career satisfaction and his depression. Robert insisted on fidelity from here on out, no matter what. They made a "no secrets" pact. They agreed to have two "dates" a week, to rediscover their mutual affection, and to spend 20 minutes each evening talking about what really mattered. Interestingly, their sex-life together was not even on their problem list.

I do not know what became of Johanna and Mike as a couple or as individuals. They moved, and I never saw either one again. I've received an annual card from Robert and Celeste for 15 years.

THE ETHICAL DECISION-MAKING PROCESS

My students maintained that I ought not to have continued to see Celeste, despite my "rationalizations" and the happy ending. I'm pleased with their response, because I believe it is best to err on the side of caution when it comes to boundary issues with clients. (These days I inform my clients up front that I do not keep "secrets," and I can't convert from couples' to individual therapy.)

My students came to two other conclusions as a result of this case study. The first is the overriding importance, even more important perhaps than the outcome, of the process that the therapist goes through in making a decision when there is an ethical dilemma or a difficult case. The process must be thoughtful and deliberate. It must include consultation or supervision, preferably with more than one colleague. They suggest a consideration of the following questions:

What are the ethical principles and issues involved? Who are the people affected? What are all the possible options? What consequences may follow from the various options? What solution seems best? Why? What personal values and feelings influenced my solution? Which types of clients "hook" me? To whom am I vulnerable in terms of losing control or objectivity? What invites me onto the slippery slope? Who might I try too hard to help? How do my motives enter into this situation? How might I follow up on the consequences of my decision?

The second conclusion my students reached as a result of this case study is that no matter the amount of training and experience, every therapist will from time to time be on the horns of a dilemma. They progressed from the common graduate student perception that ethics are clear, black/white, yes/no propositions to the recognition that there are some hard and fast rules, and many guiding principles, but not enough of these to cover every situation. They learned that there is a difference between standards and principles. We adhere to the former; we aspire to the latter. There are correct answers in the classroom, but this is much more rare in the therapy room.

My students told me they loved hearing about this case. One student thanked me, in writing, for allowing myself to be "human, respectful, and honest." Another wrote to me that exploring this case helped her to realize "how easy it is to be drawn into a client's life." She continued, "It is very difficult for me to push my ego aside and realize that I am not a client's savior and there are others who can do what I do. I appreciated your honesty. It is one thing to realize things within myself, another to put them out for peers and colleagues and especially students. Thank you for setting an example and a standard. Thank you for helping me realize that I am not alone in my struggle to be effective. This will be my challenge not just as a rookie therapist but throughout my career."

Presenting this case to graduate students and writing it up for publication reaffirms for me the importance of learning from mistakes, accepting our own fallibility, and moving on. Above all, therapists are human, too, and benefit greatly from sharing our humanity.

REFERENCES

Pittman, Frank. (1989). *Private lies: Infidelity and the betrayal of intimacy.* NY: W.W. Norton & Co.

Pope, Kenneth S., Sonne, Janet L., Holroyd, Jean. (1994). *Sexual feelings in psychotherapy: Explorations for therapists and therapists in training.* Washington, DC: American Psychological Association.

Triangulated Therapy:
Cross-Cultural Counseling

Geri Miller

SUMMARY. This article presents a case study of cross-cultural counseling involving a client and her friend, who served as a translator for the client in sessions. During three one-hour counseling sessions, a variety of ethical issues emerged. Intervention strategies and recommendations for cross-cultural counseling in this context are discussed. *[Article copies available for a fee from The Haworth Document Delivery Service: 1-800-342-9678. E-mail address: getinfo@haworthpressinc.com]*

I am a licensed psychologist in independent private practice through a local health department. I am the only mental health professional at the clinic where I volunteer a half-day a week. I am female and Caucasian. My clients are often poor women who have not had many opportunities for education. I work in a rural area which impacts my work in a number of ways: (a) women come to see me to avoid stigma (people will think they are going to the health department rather than the mental health center), (b) resources available are limited, and (c) migrant workers from Mexico are frequent clients of the health department. Women have reported seeing

Geri Miller, PhD, is Associate Professor in the Department of Human Development and Psychological Counseling at Appalachian State University. She is a Licensed Psychologist (NC), who volunteers as a psychologist one half-day a week.

Address correspondence to Geri Miller, PhD, Department of Human Development and Psychological Counseling, Edwin Duncan Hall, Appalachian State University, Boone, NC 28608.

[Haworth co-indexing entry note]: "Triangulated Therapy: Cross-Cultural Counseling." Miller, Geri. Co-published simultaneously in *Women & Therapy* (The Haworth Press, Inc.) Vol. 21, No. 3, 1998, pp. 41-47; and: *Learning from Our Mistakes: Difficulties and Failures in Feminist Therapy* (ed: Marcia Hill and Esther D. Rothblum) The Haworth Press, Inc., 1998, pp. 41-47. Single or multiple copies of this article are available for a fee from The Haworth Document Delivery Service [1-800-342-9678, 9:00 a.m. - 5:00 p.m. (EST). E-mail address: getinfo@haworthpressinc.com].

41

me because they can avoid a complicated intake process and a waiting list as well as staying in a system, the health department, where they already feel comfortable. The following case was one of my more difficult ones in that it involved cross-cultural barriers that caused me to question the ethics of my bridging them.

I saw my client for a total of three one-hour sessions within one month. She was in her mid-twenties living with her husband, her children, and her father. She was referred to counseling by a close friend who came with her to the sessions. Her friend wanted her to talk with a professional about her depression.

My client, who will be called Juanita, and her friend, who will be called Cecilia, waited for me in the crowded health department lobby for our first session. They were about 20 minutes late to the session on a day when I had clients scheduled back to back. I went out to meet them with my typical introduction of myself. Upon asking who was Juanita and did she want to follow me to the office, I realized that Juanita spoke very little English beyond "Hello." Cecilia explained that Juanita wanted her to join her in the session to be her translator. I immediately felt awkward at the realization that I would be doing an intake with someone who did not speak the same language as me. I also felt caught because I had no way of knowing the accuracy of the translation: could Cecilia capture Juanita's perspective? This was the beginning of my needing to trust Cecilia and the beginning of our triangulated counseling.

I had the presence of mind to bring a release of information with me so Juanita could sign her approval for Cecilia to sit in on our sessions to translate. As I was walking back to the office, I kept thinking, "No one ever taught me how to handle this type of situation." Numerous questions were running through my mind:

1. How am I going to evaluate what is going on when I have 30 minutes left in the session and we do not speak a common language?
2. Should I immediately refer her to a Spanish-speaking counselor?
3. How well does her friend translate?
4. Can I trust her friend?
5. Is this a potentially unhealthy triangulation?
6. Is having a session with someone who does not speak English with a translator I do not know ethical?
7. If she signs the release, how ethical is it when I do not know if she is receiving an accurate description of what it is for?
8. Is it ethical conflict or my desire for comfort which is telling me I should refer her to someone else?

As I walked to the office, I resolved I would address this session as an information gathering one where I would talk with them about counseling options and consult with another psychologist about the situation later in the day. When we entered the office, I first rearranged the seating since I was only expecting one client. I asked Juanita, via Cecilia's translation, to sign the release allowing Cecilia to translate in sessions. Both women were very friendly and appeared quite comfortable in their conversation with one another. The release was signed and I thought, "Now what?"

I began to explain my role at the health department and introduce myself professionally. I had recently heard that when working with a translator, it was a good idea to maintain eye contact with the client. However, the reality was that while I looked at Juanita, Juanita looked at Cecilia, and Cecilia looked at me. As a result, there was no eye contact between any of us. It seemed that given her interactional style and her nervousness, Juanita refused to have eye contact with me. After about ten minutes of no eye contact, I began to maintain eye contact with Cecilia with intermittent glances to Juanita. The tension in the room seemed to drop, at least it dropped within me, when I let go of the hope of a nonverbal connection of eye contact, realizing that it seemed more important to me at that time than to Juanita. I was the one who seemed hungry for some type of connection: Juanita was comfortably connected to Cecilia. I wondered if I was going to have to join their friendship somehow in order to do counseling with Juanita and if so, how right was that?

I asked why Juanita had come in for counseling and Cecilia answered for her: Cecilia said she had talked her into coming because she was worried about her. Now my anxiety went up again: Do I have a reluctant client, too? Simultaneously I questioned what I had done to deserve such a complicated situation and felt the adrenalin rush of a professional challenge.

Cecilia explained to me that Juanita felt like her younger sister and that they were very close. They were from the same town in Mexico, but did not meet until they came to this town. Because both of their husbands worked together, they met and became close friends. Cecilia explained that they did everything together and Juanita relied on her to translate in this predominantly English speaking community.

Cecilia teared up and began to cry as she spoke of her concern for Juanita. Juanita watched Cecilia carefully as she spoke, but seemed not to understand what she was saying to me. I realized Juanita probably felt as left out of the conversation as I had when Cecilia spoke to her, so I asked Cecilia to tell her what she had been telling me. I realized that either Juanita or I would feel left out of the session due to the language barrier and what I would need to do is monitor that neither one of us would be left out for long. Cecilia, not being a professional interpreter, would need to be reminded to translate for one of us in order to help us "catch up" on the conversation. I was also aware that this would be a triangulation therapy where Cecilia was our conduit to the other: any healing for Juanita would need to go through Cecilia. Finally, given the deep caring of their relationship, as expressed nonverbally through eye contact, tears, and laughter, I realized that I would also need to ask Cecilia how she felt at times in the session because of her deep care for Juanita.

I asked Cecilia to have Juanita tell me what problems had brought her in for counseling. The problems appeared relational in nature: conflicts between Juanita and her husband's relatives and conflicts between Juanita and her father. It was obvious that Cecilia was elaborating on Juanita's words given the greater amount of time spent on English than Spanish. I did not know how much I could trust Cecilia's rendition of the story, but I knew I had no other choice.

In the translation I heard symptoms of depression and questioned Juanita regarding her sleeping, eating, and sexual behaviors. There were now ten minutes left in the session and I knew I would simply have to run over into the next session in order to evaluate her depression level thoroughly. The depression sounded moderate over the last two weeks following an argument with her father. I took the opportunity to educate Juanita on the cluster symptoms of depression and talked with her about the options of medication, therapy, or a combination of both. After Cecilia translated, I could see Juanita strongly shake her head "yes" and "no." Cecilia told me Juanita would like to see me for counseling, but would never take medicine for the depression. I made a mental note to remind myself to bring up medication again if her depression continued since its usefulness might have been lost in the translation.

I began to talk with Juanita about counseling. I gave her the option of seeing me or seeing another counselor at another clinic who spoke Spanish. I had mixed feelings about working with her and a referral to a Spanish-speaking counselor would automatically release me from any ethical binds. She and Cecilia talked for a few minutes and Cecilia told me Juanita wanted to continue working with me because she felt comfortable with me even though I do not speak Spanish. We scheduled three consecutive appointments with me for counseling about her depression. They both thanked me in English as we left the session about ten minutes late. As they left my office, I thought, "Now what have I gotten myself into?"

I talked with a colleague that evening about the situation with Juanita and Cecilia. In sorting through the aspects of the situation, I decided to continue working with Juanita because that was her request. The decision seemed consistent with my commitment to the welfare of the client.

A week later they both came in for the session as did Juanita's oldest son, Michael, who was 4 years old. We all walked back to the office together and I realized I would need to bring up the appropriateness of Michael being a part of the conversation. I decided to bring it up in the office due to the language barriers (it can be difficult to hear one another in the lobby) and I was unsure if this was a cultural difference I would need to work with in the session. I initially opened the session by telling them I was glad to see both of them and asked them how they were. Juanita began to tell Cecilia about recent problems with her father. After Cecilia translated to me, I asked Juanita if she thought it was wise for her son to be present. She and Cecilia began to discuss this topic and Cecilia told me they thought Michael should play in the lobby. They told him to go to the lobby and I led him there. I was surprised at how relaxed they were with him playing in the lobby without them. Did that indicate a cultural difference, a comfort level with the health department, a trust of me, or a lax parenting style?

Once in the lobby, I realized that I did not know how much English he understood. I asked one of the desk personnel to keep a close eye on him and showed him her face, where she sat behind the counter, and pointed to him, her, and then my office. Either through the nonverbal or verbal communication he understood my message because he had the woman bring him to the office later in the session.

When I returned to the office, we discussed the recent argument between Juanita and her father. While they had always lived together, they did not have much difficulty getting along until six months ago. Since that time, the two of them reportedly argued frequently. As Juanita spoke, both she and Cecilia alternated between anger and sadness. At times I was giving Kleenex to both of them. I brought up the possibility of her father coming to counseling. After Juanita and Cecilia discussed this possibility, Cecilia told me they thought that was not a good idea; they were afraid it would only make the situation worse.

I framed the conflict in Transactional Analysis terms. While I do not consider myself a Transactional Analyst, I use an eclectic approach to counseling and Transactional Analysis seemed the most appropriate to this situation. I believed it would be effective in the counseling because it was visual, it used simple language which is easy to translate, and it focused on communication in relationships. I drew a diagram of circles showing how her father talked with Juanita in a parent-child transaction and Juanita talked with him in an adult-adult transaction. I explained that these conflicting transactions could be the cause of their conflict. They both agreed that the description of the interaction between father and daughter was accurate. While I showed them the diagram, I found myself kneeling on the floor in front of Juanita. Was I trying to have a nonverbal connection with her again and/or was I trying to diminish the power differential? I asked Juanita at the end of the session to watch her interactions with her father so we could discuss them at our next session in two weeks and determine if there were other ways she could invite an adult-adult transaction with her father.

When she came in for the last session, Juanita held herself straighter and with more confidence: even her eye contact with others had improved. I watched her direct her son to stay in the lobby and give him a dollar to use in the vending machines. What had happened to change her behavior so much? When we reached the office, Cecilia said with pride, "Juanita has a job." She explained that Juanita had obtained a housekeeping job which took her out of the house for a few hours a week. I told Juanita how different she looked and acted. Juanita smiled at the translation and said she was not depressed at all and it helped her to get away from her father and her children and have her own money. When I asked what she wanted to do about counseling, she said she did not think she needed any more.

Juanita's obtaining employment appears to be a result of both opportunity and the impact of counseling. Since becoming a mother, she had not worked outside of the home until she received counseling. Counseling became a pivotal point from which she chose to make life changes. Therefore, the changes in her behavior are a result of a synergistic relationship between her receiving counseling and obtaining employment.

I told them I would be available for counseling in the future if Juanita felt she needed it. They thanked me for my help and both of them smiled and hugged me before leaving the office. I was left with these lingering questions:

1. Did I do the "right" thing(s)?
2. Should I have insisted on a referral to a Spanish-speaking counselor?
3. Due to the unique nature of this case, how can I truly evaluate the effectiveness of therapy?

I will never know the answers to these and other questions which I think of occasionally. I do know that I did what I could live with as a therapist and hope that I did "right." I know that in the sessions there was a flow, a connectedness between the three of us that felt natural and comfortable. Lastly, I know that a young woman left therapy after three sessions feeling empowered and energized for several reasons: she obtained a job, she was validated in her struggles as a daughter and a mother, and she had a framework (Transactional Analysis) which helped her understand her struggles.

I believe there were specific factors in their friendship which allowed triangulated therapy to work. First, there was a deep respect for each other and a commitment toward one another's best interests. Second, although Juanita depended on Cecilia for translation, there was equality in their relationship. Finally, their alliance was strengthened by being two Mexican women in a predominantly Caucasian environment. This type of therapy may have failed if there was less respect, commitment, equality, and alliance in their relationship. A therapist in a similar situation would need to examine the presence of these factors within a cultural context, e.g., consult with someone familiar with the client's culture, particularly with women who experience cultural isolation.

If I had the resources, I would involve a Spanish-speaking counselor early in the therapy to make sure the client was agreeing to a translator being present. At minimum I would have a release of information and a description of me written in Spanish available to clients. I would also have some written materials in Spanish available which discuss common issues in counseling or common therapy approaches I use, such as Transactional Analysis, so that I could be assured that the translation of the terms was correct. Also, I would consult with someone familiar with the client's culture to answer my questions regarding "normal" behavior.

My suggestions to other professionals would be to consult with a professional colleague regarding unclear situations. This consultation may be particularly crucial when stretching in our work with clients. Also, the cornerstone of the welfare of the client may clarify the action to be taken as it did in this situation. I would encourage others to watch nonverbal communication carefully, be aware of cultural differences, and trust their intuition in terms of connecting with another human being. There is a genuinessness of spirit and compassion which can cross cultural and language barriers. I believe we can feel that realness in a room without a word being spoken. Within a short time, communication skills, intuition, trust, and connectedness can bring healing across cultural barriers especially in situations and times where we do not have adequate resources for counseling.

Managing Anxiety:
The Client's and Mine

Gloria Rose Koepping

SUMMARY. Helping to manage the anxiety of a client who has an anxiety disorder and managing the countertransferential anxiety of the therapist is often a challenge. This article relates the struggle of one therapist who is learning to develop her persistence into patience. *[Article copies available for a fee from The Haworth Document Delivery Service: 1-800-342-9678. E-mail address: getinfo@haworthpressinc.com]*

I've seen Rochelle (pseudonym) for 28 sessions, spread out over a period of one and a half years, encompassing six academic quarters. She initially came to see me because a man in her college class asked her to get out of her seat and give it to him. She did. Then she was angry with herself and him and wanted to be more assertive in situations like that in the future. After that first session additional concerns became apparent. Rochelle had intermittent generalized anxiety, panic attacks, social skills

Gloria Rose Koepping, PhD, is Coordinator of Psychological Services in the Counseling Center at Highline Community College in Des Moines, WA. At her college she works to retain, graduate, and employ economically and educationally disadvantaged women students.

The author wishes to thank Marge J. Koepping, MN, ARNP, for her consultation, Tracy Maynard for her editorial assistance and her therapist for her continued support of her personal and professional endeavors.

Address correspondence to Gloria Rose Koepping, Highline Community College, Counseling Center 6-10C, 2400 South 240th Street, Des Moines, WA 98198 (e-mail: gkoeppin@hcc.ctc.edu).

[Haworth co-indexing entry note]: "Managing Anxiety: The Client's and Mine." Koepping, Gloria Rose. Co-published simultaneously in *Women & Therapy* (The Haworth Press, Inc.) Vol. 21, No. 3, 1998, pp. 49-54; and: *Learning from Our Mistakes: Difficulties and Failures in Feminist Therapy* (ed: Marcia Hill and Esther D. Rothblum) The Haworth Press, Inc., 1998, pp. 49-54. Single or multiple copies of this article are available for a fee from The Haworth Document Delivery Service [1-800-342-9678, 9:00 a.m. - 5:00 p.m. (EST). E-mail address: getinfo@haworthpressinc.com].

deficits (specifically communication difficulties), depression, and disruptive family members who would call and berate her for not taking care of her grandmother, moving back home, or getting through school faster. Rochelle had problems with expressing her anger appropriately, confronting people who abused her, and a social phobia (speaking to groups in public). At this writing the social phobia has prevented her from completing a speech class that would enable her to be awarded a two year vocational degree. Rochelle meets the criteria for Generalized Anxiety Disorder, but somehow this diagnosis doesn't quite capture the extent of her difficulties. Rochelle is a 41-year-old white woman with no friends, a history of sporadic employment, and an intense self-hatred. She was medicated with Zoloft (anti-depressant) and Lorazapam (anti-anxiety medication) in the past year, and currently takes only Buspar (for anxiety).

What makes my therapeutic work with Rochelle difficult is threefold. Questions of differential and multiple diagnoses, providing a safe enough environment for therapy to occur, and improving the effectiveness of therapy are my prime concerns. First, I'm not convinced that I have the correct diagnosis. Sometimes I believe that she is depressed also, and other times I believe she exhibits elements of a personality disorder or Posttraumatic Stress Disorder. Often I think the diagnosis doesn't matter as much as decreasing her social isolation, retaining her in school, and helping her manage her anxiety long enough to get a degree and a job. (My pragmatic community college counseling center focus leaks out!) Second, I've never been able to keep her in session for more than 15-20 minutes, without her jumping up and saying, "I don't want to talk about that any more!" and leaving my office. There is not a hostile tone to her words, just an urgency that she must leave as quickly as possible. Sometimes she calls me later to apologize for her sudden exit and sometimes I have to call her after her next missed session, encouraging her to return to therapy. It would also be good to see Rochelle more often, at least once a week. In reviewing my notes, it appears that every quarter she logs more sessions than the previous quarter. Although one could interpret this as an escalating problem, I interpret it as making progress. Third, I'm not really sure my therapy with her is making any real change in her underlying problems. So what should I do differently?

There have been three critical incidents in therapy that also merit reporting. The first was about 3 months ago when she was ending spring quarter and beginning to catastrophize about getting a job. She was having difficulty with her resume, so when she asked me to review it, I took it. I then revised it on my computer and returned the edited version and a copy on disk to her at our next session. She was so taken aback and overjoyed that I could finally see her body physically relax. She had been so consumed over that piece of paper and laying it out perfectly that she couldn't concentrate on editing it herself, even though she was capable of doing so. My half-hour editing job also had the effect of softening Rochelle's attitude toward our therapy work together. She began to come to therapy more often and stay just a few minutes longer.

Although some therapists might consider editing a client's resume inappropriate in terms of therapeutic boundaries, I did not consider it so in this situation. I am by training a Counseling Psychologist, providing both personal and career counseling to my clients. Often within the flow of therapy I move from career issues (choosing a major/program, writing a resume, job interviewing) to the personal issues (anxiety, depression) which impede the daily tasks of living, working, or going to school. For me it is not uncommon nor unexpected to see the connection and work with the overlap between personal and career concerns. In fact, doing good career counseling depends upon this premise. I think editing my client's resume worked as an intervention with my client, because she too, has begun to see how her anxiety is related to her performance in class, writing a resume, or her wariness of interviews and job applications. Editing her resume also was a corrective emotional experience, because people in her family, and people (in her program) at school didn't give her the feeling of belonging and being cared for by others. Until my client resolves or decreases her anxiety, she will not be as successful as she can be in the dual worlds of school and work. I am not engaging in only personal therapy or counseling with my client, but a fluid combination of personal and career therapeutic work.

The second critical incident was offering my binoculars to Rochelle for use as a prop in her speech class. (You get the impression by now that I am desperately looking for any way I can convey my support of Rochelle's academic or personal agenda.) Again she was surprised and yet appreciative, as she took my binoculars home to practice. However, this third attempt at taking and completing a speech class was not successful. Rochelle became too anxious as the first in-class speech approached and withdrew from the course. I consoled her and myself by reminding her that this time she made it further through the class than she usually did. That counts as progress, too.

The third incident involved Rochelle bringing in an audiotape of her sister and father on the phone together and another one she tape recorded when her sister called her one night. She asked me to listen to them and tell her what I thought. When I replied that her sister sounded insincere, disrespectful, and manipulative, she exclaimed, "So you see it, too, you see what I've been talking about. Not everybody sees it. She fools them all." This led to a short but productive discussion of some of her family's dynamics. Rochelle has been more connected to me since this session, calling my voice mail or me in between sessions to leave short reports on her ongoing job search. One day she even announced, "I usually don't like women, but I like you."

I realize that we have made some headway towards her goals. She comes more often to therapy now, she stays a little longer, and she will talk about family or people at school with whom she's angry, if only for a few minutes.

I, however, am still anxious. I expected to be able to help this person get through a single speech class, to relieve her anxiety and hopelessness, to increase her frustration tolerance, and to help her befriend other people. In a year and a half, I have made some progress, but not as much as I would have liked.

I did think about trying relaxation or anxiety management techniques (hypnosis, breathing, imagery, progressive muscle relaxation, etc.) while she was in the office but I didn't feel that was appropriate without a comprehensive intake and definitive diagnosis. I'm not sure if my client needs some skills training or medication or both. Additionally we seem to go from crisis to crisis each week, and I invariably have a difficult time following up on last week's theme before she departs again. I didn't want to treat her anxiety without knowing the exact nature of her anxiety and understanding its nuances. With that information (knowing her specific symptoms and in what situations she experienced the most anxiety) I might specifically tailor a written script or a tape to send home with her. In our shortened sessions, however, I have never quite felt confident that I understood her anxiety adequately enough to begin to devise interventions in order to alleviate or reduce her symptoms. I thought it would be irresponsible to apply any relaxation technique when I didn't fully understand her anxiety and its origin.

I've also consulted with another counselor who saw my client one summer for two sessions when I wasn't working. She advised me to reinforce her compliance with the prescribed medication, allow her to go away, and then return as she felt the need to see me. She also advised me to try to remain calm, steady, and nonjudgmental. I should allow the therapeutic relationship to build and strengthen.

Surely there must be something more I can do? As I head into the fall of a new year, my client is still two classes away from graduation, and I'm not sure how to help get her there. I can't keep her in my office long enough to do much cognitive therapy for her anxiety, and she won't stay on medication long enough to get some real relief (I suspect this is due to poverty, and her accompanying sense of pride more so than any noncompliance on her part). Although my client has had trials of various medications in the distant past, she more recently says she doesn't have the money for medication, and has to get funds from her mother to pay her monthly bills. Periodically she discusses bankruptcy and cries about her charge card debt. All attempts to problem-solve with her about inexpensive or free sources for her medication were rebuffed. Maybe I could have pursued working with a psychiatrist to find a more advantageous medication? Would that have increased her willingness to utilize medication? A nurse practitioner I consulted suggested speaking with her M.D. about a trial of Inderal. This drug would block her sympathetic nervous system response and allow her to give a speech without the accompanying physical responses. As long as she can tolerate the medication and afford it, that would be an additional solution I can offer my client next quarter.

I'm still embarrassed, however, that she leaves my office after 20 minutes, 25 on a good day. Afterwards, I usually run down the hall to get another therapist to reassure me that it's not me, it's *her* anxiety. I still have a hard time not personalizing her anxious reactions to therapy. When I meet with her, I feel inadequate as a therapist. Sometimes her anxiety adds to mine. Usually I am able to make people feel at ease, and they develop a working relationship with me easily. That is not the case with Rochelle. I understand I need to be patient with her process, but I am not patient with myself. I used to think I was a patient person. I *know* I am a persistent person. But it takes more than average patience to be a therapist. I'm still taking too much responsibility for her progress.

What have I learned from this client? In retrospect, I believe that I should have sought out consultation earlier in our therapeutic relationship and from more therapists than I initially did. I'm not sure that would have helped our therapy, but it probably would have made me feel more competent than I did. Most of us only consult with people that are easily accessible in our workplace, and I would advise other therapists to seek out consultants as well who have different experiences and perspectives from our usual fare. In this way more explanations or strategies might appear. Remember not to forget those medical consultations as well. If I had not consulted a nurse practitioner, I wouldn't have known of a medication alternative for my client's class presentation anxiety. I'd also recommend bringing clients like this up in your own personal therapy when working with them touches on your own issues. Maybe my anxiety about being a competent therapist contributed to my client's anxiety in this instance.

In working with Rochelle I realized I have a therapeutic edge, a place I push up against and can't go any further, at least right now. That edge is my patience. I have such a need to understand everything right now and fix it that I sometimes forget to let my client set the pace. I am impatient. I want to find a technique, get a drug, make her feel at ease.

I want to use my persistence to be more patient. With continued self-monitoring, additional consultation with colleagues, and my personal therapy, I hope to develop better anxiety management of my own, not personalize my client's anxieties, and remember the responsibility boundaries of my therapeutic relationships. I consider all of this, and wonder what will happen as I await her return in the fall.

The Client Re-Visited:
A Second Look at a Near Failure

Rascha Levinson

SUMMARY. The author describes her treatment of a difficult client, a woman who was angry at everyone almost continuously, who put down therapy even as she was making progress. The therapist discusses her countertransference feelings with this client, and some thoughts about the nature of "mistakes." In writing this article, the author discovered that the treatment was not as much of a failure as she had remembered initially. *[Article copies available for a fee from The Haworth Document Delivery Service: 1-800-342-9678. E-mail address: getinfo@ haworthpressinc.com]*

Nicole was a tall, willowy brunette with hazel eyes, in her middle thirties, white, well-educated and very verbal. She was extremely angry and constantly "expressed her anger" which she felt was "healthy." She was married to an accountant and had two daughters, eight and ten years old. She was one of my most difficult clients. Her continuous anger and complaints triggered my fears that I was an inadequate therapist and that

Rascha Levinson, CSW, BCD, has been in private practice as a feminist therapist in New York City and Westchester for 27 years. She has been a member of, and held various offices in, AWP, FTI, AHP, NYSCSWP and WPRS. She has one daughter and two grandsons. In the last fifteen years she has given papers and workshops at the New School in New York City and at national feminist conferences in the areas of relationships and creativity.

Address correspondence to Rascha Levinson, 75 Sunset Drive, Ossining, NY 10562.

[Haworth co-indexing entry note]: "The Client Re-Visited: A Second Look at a Near Failure." Levinson, Rascha. Co-published simultaneously in *Women & Therapy* (The Haworth Press, Inc.) Vol. 21, No. 3, 1998, pp. 55-61; and: *Learning from Our Mistakes: Difficulties and Failures in Feminist Therapy* (ed: Marcia Hill and Esther D. Rothblum) The Haworth Press, Inc., 1998, pp. 55-61. Single or multiple copies of this article are available for a fee from The Haworth Document Delivery Service [1-800-342-9678, 9:00 a.m. - 5:00 p.m. (EST). E-mail address: getinfo@haworthpressinc.com].

55

she would leave therapy because of this. I was often frustrated by her defensive maneuvers.

Nicole would talk a great deal about her anxieties and her depression but, when I asked a question or tried to go deeper into the problem, she would say that her period was due, or that everything was really O.K. She would frequently interrupt when I talked. Often she would say something and pause. When I would then start to say something, she would cut me off. When I reflected back her feelings, she would say, "No, it's not like that" and modify what I had said or go off on a tangent.

All of this was very frustrating and made me angry. I felt inept. Even though I could see intellectually that she was, and needed to be, very well-defended, that she was fearful of revealing herself and of trusting me, I felt angry, afraid and rejected. At the same time she was telling me things: she talked about her mother, who was so depressed, who never helped Nicole with her problems. Every time Nicole came to her mother for help, they would wind up talking about mother's problems. Nicole talked about her father, who was always busy at work making money. He adored Nicole's younger sister, who was a "genius" and graduated MIT with honors, but he never knew what class Nicole was in.

After many of these beginning sessions, I would write myself questions about what I wanted to ask Nicole to get "working." I rarely, if ever, asked those questions because I was too intimidated. Nicole would interrupt, contradict, and I would fall silent. After a while I adopted the stance of simply listening in a supportive way to whatever she was saying.

One evening, after Nicole had been in treatment for six months, she called me saying she had suddenly started to tremble and shake for no reason. Then she said it was because she was menstruating. As I stayed on the phone with her, saying that this was a frightening experience and that it must feel awful, she listened. We were on the phone for about 15 minutes. After this time, Nicole began to feel better and felt ready to hang up. I assured her that we would talk more about this if she needed to at her next session. This was a breakthrough. She had reached out for help when she was frightened and vulnerable, something she hadn't done until now. She allowed me to come closer.

Nicole began talking more about her difficulties with her husband: he was self-centered, immature and unable to empathize with her feelings. It took me a while to understand that she was projecting these qualities onto him. They were the qualities she had experienced in her mother. Nicole was often in a rage with Derrick, yelling and screaming. After two or three sessions of her complaining about Derrick, I suggested we have a joint session with him, but Nicole said she didn't want to. "No good will come of it," she said gloomily.

Nicole and Derrick went for a vacation that winter. When Nicole came for her first session after she got her bill for that month, she immediately and angrily started talking about my charging for her missed session. I had not told her that I would charge for missed sessions when she first came, she said. I was manipulative and arbitrary. I said she was right, that I should have told her in the beginning. It was my mistake. She kept on angrily. I asked how she was feeling. "Mad," she said. I then asked who had done something like that to her. "That's irrelevant!" she snapped. At this point her anger seemed to be increasing. I asked her what would make her feel better. Nicole said in a more reflective tone that she had not thought about that. We talked some more and were able to come to a solution with Nicole in a calmer mood.

At the same time that all this was going on, there would be times when I could see the situations Nicole was telling me about, her complaints, accusations, anger, through her eyes. Her parents had been critical, as well as self-involved and unloving. This led me to feelings of unconditional love for her. I was not able to maintain these feelings for any length of time because they would be interrupted by her bursts of extreme anger at anyone from Derrick to people driving on the roads. She continually called Derrick a selfish moron and an idiot.

One day Nicole came in and told me about an incident that had occurred over the weekend. She prefaced the story with, "This is ridiculous, totally ridiculous. I'm so moronic to get upset about this." She launched into a story of how their roof needed to be repaired and the repairman, a very slight, very young-looking man was up on their pitched roof when she got back from the supermarket on Saturday. She immediately had a strong visual image of this "child," as she called him, falling off the roof and dying of injuries from his fall. This image upset her terribly. The company would sue them for millions of dollars and the roof repair was expensive. Nicole told her husband, who dismissed this fantasy, said she was "crazy." She then yelled at him. She was in a rage because he did not care if she was upset and made no effort to comfort her. I said that it seemed to me that Derrick, and then she herself, belittled the incident which had upset her very much. It made her very anxious that the roofer might get hurt. He really was a very young person, a child almost. Derrick, as so often happened, was unable to empathize and her anxiety turned to rage. I wondered if this wasn't a pattern: Nicole got anxious; husband could not understand; she felt alone and uncared for and let out her rage at him. Nicole had picked a husband who was unable to comfort her when she was upset just like her mother. By attacking him with anger and put-downs, she let out all the pain she had had to repress as a child. However, when she screamed at Derrick and called him names, he got furious and even less able or willing to comfort her. Like many men, he had a hard time hearing her to begin with and then his anger made it totally impossible.

While telling me this story, Nicole maintained eye contact with me throughout. This was the first time this had happened. By the end of the story, I had feelings of unconditional love for her, feeling the pain of the uncared-for child that was so large a part of this woman.

As she was leaving, Nicole said suddenly, "I don't want to go home. Can I sleep here?" I was struck dumb by the remark and then she was out the door. The next session she dismissed the remark as a joke. The session after that Nicole said she was unhappy with the way therapy was going. This was a pattern that discouraged me every time it happened. Each time I thought I could move ahead, I allowed her to intimidate me.

The next week she told me about an old memory that had surfaced. She was very young, about three, and she and her parents were in a playground. It must have been the weekend. She fell from something–maybe a jungle gym–and the breath was knocked out of her. She hurt all over and cried frantically. Mother and father rushed over, picked her up and fussed over her but, Nicole said, "I just wanted them to put me down. There wasn't any comfort in their holding me." I said, "That must have been awful. You were upset and hurt and even when they were there and wanted to comfort you, they couldn't." I also wondered how they had let her climb so high that she could fall and hurt herself. She was very young. Nicole said bitterly, "I'll bet they weren't even watching me. My mother was probably complaining about something to my father, wanting him to help her." I said, "So when Derrick doesn't help you when you're upset, it must feel to you just like your parents who didn't take care of you, couldn't comfort you, and you let out all the pain and rage you must have felt as a child to Derrick, when you couldn't let it out to your parents. And it sounds like your mother had a hard time getting attention and caring from your father, just as you do from Derrick."

Nicole listened to me without interrupting. At times an angry expression flitted across her face, but she did not say anything. When I had finished, there was silence for a minute; then she changed the subject.

Nicole's 35th birthday arrived and she convinced her husband to go hiking and mountain climbing with her in the west as a birthday present. When they returned, Nicole was exhilarated, said for the first time she felt "solid"–a very different feeling than she had ever had. She also had decided to learn how to hang glide, something she had always wanted to do but had been too anxious to do.

A few sessions later she said she felt she did not need to come to therapy anymore. The one who still had problems was her husband. This felt like the final straw after repeated rejections. I was so angry that I was able to say that it wasn't just Derrick; she still had work to do. "What?" she said, challenging me. I talked about her anger, which still flared up almost daily, that she was not supportive of her husband, still called him names and belittled him at every turn. Her face blanched but then she gave me a long list of reasons why therapy wasn't working, all of which she had used throughout therapy. A wave of extreme fatigue washed over me. Working with Nicole was taxing. I felt that termination at this point was premature because Nicole had not really integrated the changes she had made on a conscious level. I sensed that she wasn't going to continue, but I was too tired from the constant rejection to say anymore. I decided to end on a positive note. We did that, spending the next few sessions in a termination process. She had been in therapy for a year and a half.

At the time Nicole terminated, I felt that her treatment was a very partial success, almost a failure. Now, after poring over my notes, rethinking her case, I believe it was more of a success than I had previously recognized, though still only a partial one. I think about what I did that I would like to change and what I did that I think helped Nicole. Nicole made many comments that I could have explored further. When she would interrupt, or contradict me, or say her depression was because her period was due, or that everything was really O.K., I could have remarked on how often she said these things and wondered what she was feeling at the time. When she would talk about her anger, I did not ask, "What about that made you so angry?" I have said that to other clients, so why couldn't I say that to her? I think it was because she interrupted, contradicted and persistently complained that therapy (and by extension, the therapist) was not helping. One of the rewards of doing therapy is that we get to feel helpful. It was painful not to get that reward.

These defensive maneuvers stimulated intense countertransference feelings. I felt, under constant threat of abandonment, that she would leave and so prove me an inadequate therapist. I felt not only this present-oriented fear, but the same fears going back to my childhood, in their childhood forms. What child has not had fears of abandonment and of being inadequate?–and every therapist was once a child.

Because of the difficulties Nicole presented, I went for consultation twice. In the first consult I was told that I needed to confront Nicole's behavior. For example, her yelling at Derrick when she was feeling anxious and needy instead of getting in touch with her own feelings and telling him about them. I was not able to use the suggestion. I went for a second consult. It was suggested to me that I teach her self-hypnosis for times when she became anxious. I wasn't able to do that. I didn't really agree with that suggestion. I think now that the reason I was unable to benefit from these consults was that, although we touched on my counter-transference issues, I needed to go into them at a greater depth. Since this was such a core issue, additional supervision might have helped me with Nicole and with other clients. Countertransference feelings, like transfer-ence feelings, take time to work through and two consults weren't enough time. My childhood fears of my father's criticism and anger were triggered by Nicole's often angry and critical stance. Her off-and-on dissatisfaction with therapy and talk of leaving echoed what I thought my father must have felt and which made me afraid he would leave the family.

Another reason why I did not do as much exploration and interpretation as I might have was my difficulty at this point in combining an intensely supportive approach with what seemed, from this point of view, to be negative interpretations. When Nicole would say how awful Derrick had been over the weekend, it felt as though pointing out that she could have talked to him about what she felt would be received by her as a negative, critical remark and I didn't know how to say that in a way that she would receive positively. I could have said "I feel that almost anything I say would be too much for you."

This brings me to the question of mistakes. Was it a series of mistakes that I did not explore her anger, many of her defensive comments? Mis-takes are often in the eye of the beholder, that is, different people who operate from different contexts often have conflicting ideas as to whether a particular action is a mistake or not. For example, I had another client whose feelings had never been validated or even talked about by her alcoholic parents. When she terminated with me to go to college in another city, she started with a new therapist. This therapist phoned me and let me know that every time my name came up, the client would cry. She clearly felt I had made the client excessively attached to me, that I had done something very wrong to produce this behavior. I felt that this client had come to me completely cut off from her own feelings and I was probably the first person in her life who accepted and supported those feelings. It seems to me that her grief at losing her relationship with me (though by her own decision) was a good sign. She was able to mourn appropriately at losing an important relationship, rather than not feeling anything at the loss.

Because I knew the client's context, I could see that her mourning the relationship was progress, not a mistake on my part. Even if she were aware of this context, the new therapist still might have considered that I had made an error. My intuition told me her orientation held that, above all, the therapist must remain objective and detached. In this instance, we are dealing with more than one context.

Over the course of therapy, which may last several years, it is much harder to decide which interventions are the right ones, the ones that produce change. We are trained and have experiences which help to guide us to ask and say helpful things. But, finally, the therapist does not know whether a given question at a specific time is the right one. You take a risk.

I believe the most helpful thing I did was to listen to Nicole: simply to listen, and then to listen in a more and more supportive way. I feel that my support, my empathy, and at times my unconditional love, were the factors that enabled this woman occasionally to drop her critical, rageful, self-sufficient persona, to let go of the wariness, the continual put-downs that held me at arm's length. In addition to my countertransference fears, it may have been my intuition that kept me silent. I had, especially at the beginning, a very strong feeling of "not being able to get in," of there being no room for me to say anything. I have had this with other clients, but rarely as powerfully as with Nicole. Not pushing Nicole to explore her anger and negativity may have helped her to trust me and to let go of her defenses on many occasions. It may have even kept her in therapy.

I interpreted Nicole's rage as a cover for her pain, pointed out that her needs were not being met currently, had not been met in the past. My listening and this kind of interpretation, I believe, facilitated those moments of unconditional love. After these experiences, she was able to begin to control her attacks on her husband, recovered an important memory and generally was able to hear me better. Going mountain climbing (which can be seen as symbolic as well as real) enabled her to feel "solid" which she had never experienced before. It is interesting that she then felt finished with therapy. Was that because she felt whole or because this experience frightened her back into withdrawal?

In summary, this was therapy with a client who was extremely difficult, wanting to, and yet terrified of, letting me come close enough to facilitate some change. I was not sure that she could sustain the changes she had initiated, although sometimes a small variation in behavior will lead to a much larger change in the end. At least she had gotten a taste of what being nurtured was like and how being "solid" felt. My hope is that this would enable her to return to therapy if she felt the need.

Where, Oh Where,
Has the Therapeutic Alliance Gone?
Disquieting Log-Jams
in the Therapeutic Relationship

Marcia Perlstein

SUMMARY. Therapists find it difficult to talk about impasses or failed therapies, yet doing so can be quite constructive. This article describes three categories in terms of the therapist's countertransference process: (1) that which ends in a "premature termination"; (2) that which stays stuck for an excruciatingly long period of time until the therapist initiates termination; (3) that which stays stuck for a long period of time where the client initiates termination. *[Article copies available for a fee from The Haworth Document Delivery Service: 1-800-342-9678. E-mail address: getinfo@haworthpressinc.com]*

I want to/I don't want to talk about impassses in the therapy office. I have them; they bother me. Knowing that we all have them and seldom talk about them doesn't make the pain any less or the cycle of feelings I go

---

Marcia Perlstein, MA, MFCC, has been a practicing psychotherapist in Berkeley and San Francisco, California since 1967. She is currently Director of North Berkeley Psychiatric Institute and the Alternative Family Project, San Francisco, California as well.

Address correspondence to Marcia Perlstein, 1806 Martin Luther King Jr. Way, Berkeley, CA 94709 (e-mail: scraggs3@ccnet.com).

[Haworth co-indexing entry note]: "Where, Oh Where, Has the Therapeutic Alliance Gone? Disquieting Log-Jams in the Therapeutic Relationship." Perlstein, Marcia. Co-published simultaneously in *Women & Therapy* (The Haworth Press, Inc.) Vol. 21, No. 3, 1998, pp. 63-68; and: *Learning from Our Mistakes: Difficulties and Failures in Feminist Therapy* (ed: Marcia Hill and Esther D. Rothblum) The Haworth Press, Inc., 1998, pp. 63-68. Single or multiple copies of this article are available for a fee from The Haworth Document Delivery Service [1-800-342-9678, 9:00 a.m. - 5:00 p.m. (EST). E-mail address: getinfo@haworthpressinc.com].

through any easier. I go through a process akin to a more expressive fight with loved ones I'm in relationship with: family, lovers, close friends. Akin, but different since as therapist, I honor boundaries. With clients, I save the ugly parts for talking and thinking and feeling to myself, wanting not to dump my process on the client's psyche during the client's hour. I'm clear that that's the way to do it. Sometimes I raise the issue in a peer consultation group or seek consultation from a trusted colleague. I even have countertransference around other therapists' impasses. I was once on the editorial board of a professional journal. I rejected an article by a colleague speaking of an impasse she had experienced as the client of a respected colleague. It felt too volatile and "unprofessional"; the client/ therapist's feelings were too raw. I was accused of not having courage; of censorship. I had thought of it as sensitivity. I was outvoted and the article published.

I'm going to describe my countertransference process with three categories of impasses: (1) that which ends in a "premature termination" (2) that which stays stuck and goes on and on and on. . . . until I initiate termination (3) that which stays stuck and goes on and on and on. . . . until the client initiates termination.

(1) I see premature terminations as slammed doors; impasses with no opportunities for turning things around. Sometimes they follow a hard session or even one where I made a mistake. Generally in thinking about my error afterwards and coming to a level of understanding, I look forward to the next session where I can indicate my error, we can both learn and go on from there. In this best case scenario I feel I have modelled accountability and reflection with an openness to change. Almost always the therapy is moved a notch to another level.

Occasionally, the client doesn't come in for that next session and the final contact is a message on my voice mail. As is standard for most of us, I'm opposed to having a therapy process conclude on voice mail; instead, I encourage the client to come in for a wrap-up session. For me the therapeutic failure occurs when the client won't come in. I try to indicate on the phone that I support their right to the choice of terminating therapy but would like an opportunity for closure. When the client still refuses, I wait a period of time and then send a short note with the final bill.

My most recent premature termination occurred with a client I'd only seen twice who began by seeking long-term treatment. In the last session we had she indicated wanting to plan a trip to see her only sister but that she had a deep fear of flying which has gotten worse over time; and her fear had completely stopped her from visiting for the past four years. I indicated that part of the fear could be treated with guided visualizations if she felt that that might be useful and the rest through continuing to understand and deal with her embattled relationship with her sister. I explained about the use of these visualizations in a variety of instances ranging from common phobias to work with chronic illness. I gave her examples of visualizations where she might feel held and safe (such as floating on clouds) as opposed to fearful. She indicated that until she got to know me better she wouldn't feel safe utilizing that technique. I told her I understood and wouldn't bring it up again; that, after a period of time if she decided it might be useful that she could let me know, otherwise, we could let it go entirely. We spent the rest of the session on her very complicated relationship with her mother. She left indicating that she'd see me the next week.

Her phone message which came in after 11:00 P.M. two nights before her next scheduled session indicated that she was going to find another way to work on her fear of flying issues and discontinue seeing me. The next day when I called her I encountered her private voicemail. I left a message indicating that I understood her choice but would also like to give her an opportunity to meet as planned and to turn the scheduled session into a wrap-up meeting. She told my voicemail that she had already made other plans for that time. I haven't heard from her since.

This is a fairly typical premature termination. My countertransference is that, though the magnitude of this is relatively minor, since we'd barely begun working together, every interrupted process causes me frustration, reflection, feelings of mini-abandonment and being misunderstood. I do understand that she got extremely frightened and needed the safety and personal empowerment that comes with choosing to leave. Part is the healthy exercise of choice; part is simply acting out the fear through flight. However brief our contact, I will put this in the therapeutic failure column and learn greater caution in offering techniques when someone first raises an issue. While some people come to me having heard that I play a very active role in therapy sessions, I need to leave more space for them to request a particular kind of assistance. In this case, it is also clear that the other side of the countertransference is that I truly love another opportunity to keep learning, difficult as it may feel at times.

(2) There are (a) certain impasses which build steadily and sometimes culminate in a confrontation; (b) some which are like a chronic block which gets re-enacted each session in a similar fashion; and, finally (c) others in which the client acts out towards the therapy through frequent missed or interrupted sessions.

As therapists we each have varying degrees of success with each type depending on our training, personality and "trigger areas." I do well with those in category "a" and have an unusual amount of patience with "b"; however, I am most ineffective at handling "c," acting out towards the therapy, when I can't help the client express the feelings preferably instead of, or even along with, acting them out. I work very well with clients who act out in other arenas of their lives, particularly adolescents and substance abusers; but over time if the acting out occurs towards the therapy but not in the therapy office, I eventually initiate a termination. I always bring up the subject non-punitively; offer appropriate other resources and referrals; and encourage one or several sessions for closure. I usually put it in terms of helping them have the words and music match. Since they are not wanting to come; rather than feel bad about themselves, let me help them "talk with their feet"; leave this situation and move on to one which might better suit them at this time. I indicate that they are most welcome to return in the future if they desire to make use of my services.

I have to say a number of things about this. First, I never take any impasses lightly and before coming to a decision to initiate a termination I leave no stone unturned in trying to break through the impasse and get the treatment moving. Secondly, I don't come to this decision with many cases; perhaps a half dozen since I began practicing in 1967. Finally, in three cases over the years, my raising the issue of the possibility of termination has resulted in a breakthrough of the impasse, dramatic enough that therapy has not merely continued but movement has been stimulated.

The most dramatic example of the above occurred many years ago with a young man in his thirties. He had a number of violence and drug issues. His life was in jeopardy after several accidents and he periodically struck his wife. He continued drinking heavily and using a variety of illegal drugs as well. He refused to participate in any group situation, recovery or twelve step program. I continued seeing him, feeling that we had some therapeutic alliance and that if he had a successful experience in treatment with me that he might eventually be willing to expand the circle of help he could avail himself of. For awhile he came relatively regularly, several times a week. Then his wife left him and he responded by disappearing from therapy. She abandoned him; he left treatment. Fearing for his safety and the safety of others, I called him regularly to encourage him to return. I planned to move him into a more comprehensive program than I could provide by myself. When he came back he began sobbing and saying he did not know what he would do if I "kicked him out." I hadn't even raised the issue. He realized that he couldn't, and we couldn't, continue such limited treatment. I built on his motivation in the moment–he had truly bottomed out–and said that I would continue working with him but now must insist that he get additional support. He agreed to get into a recovery program. As dramatic as his bottom was, so was the change. He eventually got clean and sober, began working in his uncle's business (and now runs it entirely) and has a new girlfriend.

(3) There are some positive terminations initiated by clients in response to impasses. Other impasses are troublesome as they occur and leave a dissatisfied sense of the treatment for both the client and me. I try to turn client initiated terminations that occur in the office into opportunities and to help the client consider other options. However, often because our therapy has not worked out, the client carries a generalized distrust and is unwilling to try working with another therapist or treatment mode such as group therapy. This feeling is often accompanied by a good deal of anger and a sense that there has been a heavy investment of time, energy and money which has not paid off.

Often impasses can be broken through a cataclysmic event which occurs outside the therapy office and therapy resumes on a deeper level. (This was true in the example above); somehow the stuck molecules shift and new openings for interpretation and change can be found. In other instances, the same event stimulates movement completely out of treatment. Other times, the client's termination appears to come from nowhere; though the impasse has been building, the time the client chooses to terminate seems no different than the sessions before. In these instances, I am noticing small, incremental progress but the client either doesn't experience it or finds the pace far too slow.

My countertransference around client initiated terminations varies. Sometimes I feel the same cluster of failure, mini-abandonment and missed opportunities as in a premature termination. Other times I feel I did my best and am slightly relieved not to have to continue participating in a treatment which simply had stopped progressing and which I knew no way to turn around–even with consultation. I don't usually give myself permission to feel relief, but nevertheless, in some instances, that is my predominant human emotion.

One instance doesn't quite fit any of the above categories, but really was an impasse which deserves mention. I describe this here because although the process wasn't therapy–it was the supervision of an intern– there was a genuine transference and countertransference both during the supervision sessions, throughout the impasses and through the termination process. Both during supervision sessions and throughout the termination, however, I will say, that though the direction is that described above, the magnitude was restrained and graceful because we both maintained the professional container. Nevertheless the process was painful for both of us and the resolution–transfer to another supervisor initiated by the intern–

was graceful. It was also very empowering for the intern and a very special learning experience for me. Though a hard-working student in some ways, her areas of difficulty triggered identification in me of my own weaknesses. No matter how I packaged my feedback, she often experienced it as criticism. We tried talking about the difficulties and would have a few weeks of productive, tension-free meeting; then, the problem would begin repeating itself and building. Finally, she decided to find another supervisor. I was very proud of how she handled it and we did far better in the working our way out of the supervisor/intern relationship than we had done remaining in it. Her next experience was a far more positive one and she is now fully licensed.

In closing, I must write a brief summary of my process in writing this article. I wanted to address this issue from the moment I was invited to. However, hand in glove with my interest was my uneasiness. Though very busy with other projects, I made arrangements to get a realistic deadline so that I could spend some time reflecting, writing and revising. Then I found, even with the extra time when the deadlines for my other projects had come and gone, I was having difficulty writing this. I feared that I would be typecast as the therapist who shared too much of the negative truths in my own process. I'd be seen as self-indulgent, not professional enough and not "distant" enough from the client to be useful. Then I reread this and realized that other therapists had experienced many of the issues I was describing and might seek the opportunity to begin an open dialogue. Thus, I invite any colleagues with the inclination to do so, to contact me. Now that I've completed this article, I'm appreciative of an experience which enabled me to own and examine impasses in the therapeutic process.

Meanings and Implications of Failure in Therapy

Jeanne Adleman
Marny Hall
Natalie Porter

SUMMARY. In a series of informal discussions stretching over several months, three veteran therapists tackled the theme of therapeutic failure. Their observations, subsequently transcribed and edited,

Jeanne Adleman, MA, born in 1919, was drawn into women's liberation movements by her daughters and believes in a feminism grounded in awareness of racial and class oppression, not only sexism. She is co-editor with Gloria Enguidanos of *Racism in the Lives of Women: Testimony, Theory, and Guides to Antiracist Practice.* She is a member and past Chair of the Feminist Therapy Institute, serves on the Advisory Board of Gay and Lesbian Outreach to Elders, and maintains an active practice in San Francisco as a consultant specializing in Feminist Therapy.
Marny Hall, PhD, LCSW, is a lesbian feminist psychotherapist who has played and worked in the San Francisco Bay Area for the last 25 years. Researcher and author, she is the editor of *Sexualities*, and the author of *The Lavender Couch: A Consumer's Guide to Psychotherapy for Lesbians and Gay Men*, and of *The Lesbian Love Companion: How to Survive Everything from Heartthrob to Heartbreak.* She is a member of the editorial board of the New York University Gay and Lesbian Series.
Natalie Porter, PhD, is Academic Dean of Clinical Psychology, California School of Professional Psychology-Alameda. She has been active in feminist psychology for twenty years and has written primarily about feminist, antiracist supervision and training issues and feminist ethics in psychology. She is co-editor with Hannah Lerman of *Feminist Ethics in Psychotherapy.*
Address correspondence to Natalie Porter, PhD, CSPP-Alameda, 1005 Atlantic Avenue, Alameda, CA 94501.

[Haworth co-indexing entry note]: "Meanings and Implications of Failure in Therapy." Adleman, Jeanne, Marney Hall, and Natalie Porter. Co-published simultaneously in *Women & Therapy* (The Haworth Press, Inc.) Vol. 21, No. 3, 1998, pp. 69-100; and: *Learning from Our Mistakes: Difficulties and Failures in Feminist Therapy* (ed: Marcia Hill and Esther D. Rothblum) The Haworth Press, Inc., 1998, pp. 69-100. Single or multiple copies of this article are available for a fee from The Haworth Document Delivery Service [1-800-342-9678, 9:00 a.m. - 5:00 p.m. (EST). E-mail address: getinfo@haworthpressinc.com].

69

draw from the literature of treatment outcome, the papers presented in this volume, and their own firsthand experience with foot-in-mouth blunders, client-therapist mismatches, and countertransference quandaries. The three discussants consider the ways in which the notion of failure is embedded in both the theory and practice of psychotherapy, and explore the ways in which this failure narrative shapes the experience of both clients and therapists. *[Article copies available for a fee from The Haworth Document Delivery Service: 1-800-342-9678. E-mail address: getinfo@haworthpressinc.com]*

CONSIDERING "ENDINGS" OF THERAPY

I will reflect upon "goings" in therapy, rather than on "failures." What did I learn? I learned as many questions as answers.

I expect perfection from myself

- how can I become perfect?
- what can I do with perfect?
- the idea that I am not perfect fills me with joy and exhaustion . . .

I anticipate heroism

- living woman's myth of service to all
- the challenge: "Do you dare to convert this suffering?"

I recall personal deficit

- I lack empathy
- I cannot fix everything
- I cannot find an excuse for . . .

I learned not to expect that a void in one person can be filled by the presence of another; that awareness of the abyss is not a cause for terminal panic. But how do I examine a stance of "do less than I can"? How do I know when I'm standing on shaky ground? How do I recognize breathlessness of the spirit?

–E. Kitch Childs[1]

MARNY: I think the papers in this [volume] are very interesting. Together with the [volume's] concept they stimulated a number of thoughts that perhaps we can use as a framework for our discussion. What became evident from reading the papers was that failure is a very relative matter. My guess is that there's often a great discrepancy between what clients think they have gotten out of therapy and what therapists think they have provided for clients. There's a great deal of research that seems to reinforce that. When clients are polled about the results of therapy they often state results different from the results therapists claim they've provided.[2]

I propose that rather than discuss the papers individually, why don't we discuss them in terms of a collective perspective–as illustrative of the way that therapists are trained to anticipate and evaluate failure?

NATALIE: Sounds good. Keep going . . .

MARNY: Professional journals, training courses, and even our own anecdotal reports emphasize effective therapeutic strategies and successful outcomes. But unless we are supervising students, we rarely hear another common theme, that is, how we have misunderstood or failed to help our clients. Yet I suspect that even those of us who are not students spend a substantial amount of time analyzing our mistakes or worrying about therapy outcomes. In other words, running parallel to our success stories is another, more private, story–a narrative of failure.

NATALIE: Can you explain what you mean by a narrative?

MARNY: A preexisting story line. For example, before any of the authors of the papers even met the clients they describe, they had, through their training, acquired a developed story about themselves and their power to make blunders. The story may go something like this: I am capable of making all kinds of mistakes; as a result, therapy may be derailed and the client's progress jeopardized; if I cannot recoup, the damage may be irreparable. In other words, therapists are primed to sort client-therapist interactions into successes or failures. An event as insignificant as a yawn can activate a therapist's failure narrative.

JEANNE: Are you saying that they and we are all programmed to respond in the same way to certain cues?

MARNY: No. I think the failure narrative varies from therapist to therapist. For some therapists, it could be triggered by absence of
rapport; for others, lack of insight. For some, the failure narrative might be activated by therapy that goes on too long; for
others, by therapy that doesn't go on long enough. I think the
content of each therapist's failure narrative is different. I also
think it varies among schools of therapy, and between seasoned
and novice therapists, as well as between micro and macro
levels. For example, wouldn't at least some of the articles have
been just as rich and diverse if the authors had focused on one
oops-filled session instead of describing an entire course of
treatment?

JEANNE: But then it would be the session, not the entire therapy, that
would be seen as a failure.

NATALIE: What is the value/purpose of this "failure narrative"?

MARNY: I think that this is what we might explore. What does the failure
narrative do for the therapists; how it operates; how therapists
acquire it, what purposes it serves; how experience modifies it;
the ways the failure narrative of feminist therapists differs from
that of more traditional therapists. I think if we became more
conscious of its operations, we would be less vulnerable to
it–perhaps even be able to tweak it in directions that might
benefit us or our clients. Ahhh . . . but you see I've just tried to
trade a failure narrative for a success narrative. I hope we can
refrain from that during our discussion. The deep issue I want
to pursue is not "treatment failure" but, rather, how does the
failure *narrative* shape the therapist and her role.

NATALIE: Do you see the failure narrative as positive or negative, as
interfering with or promoting the therapy process?

MARNY: I'm ambivalent. I think it serves a lot of very positive functions. On the other hand I think it often paralyzes therapists and
perhaps impedes the therapy. But let me describe first what I
consider to be the function of the therapy narrative.

    One of the functions of the failure narrative is the role
indoctrination of fledgling therapists. I remember being exposed as a young therapist to some horror stories about the
power abuses that Freud and his contemporary, Fleiss, perpe-

trated on Freud's client, Emma. I remember learning that therapists have power to do great ill, to hurt their clients. I also remember hearing stories about abuse: therapists sleeping with their clients; the kinds of aversive therapies gays were exposed to; lobotomies and shock treatment. These stories came together in my mind as a picture of a therapist: a person who could do very good deeds or who could also do bad deeds. In other words, a therapist was a person with great power who could wield that power in either direction.

So the failure narrative, I think, indoctrinates beginning therapists, who don't feel really powerful, to feel more powerful.

NATALIE: So the negative aspect of the conventional failure narrative is that it can create a sense of grandiosity in a therapist: "Wow, I really can be powerful and in a role that inhibits people from questioning me or inhibits my needing to question myself." What can be positive about this aspect of the narrative, however, is that if therapists are aware of the tremendous power they have, they may refrain from certain hurtful acts, such as boundary violations. I believe certain violations of clients occur when therapists don't take themselves or their roles seriously enough, when they deny their power.

THE FAILURE NARRATIVE AS BENEFICIAL TO THERAPISTS

NATALIE: I become concerned when therapists–women therapists included–who, in attempting to view themselves as egalitarian, refuse to acknowledge the power differential that is present as a function of privilege, whether class privilege, status differences, or the power of being seen as the "expert."

MARNY: Another positive effect of the failure narrative is as part of the feedback loop. For example if I feel I've made a mistake in a session in that I've been too advice-giving, intrusive, or judgmental, chances are I'll reconsider my position, particularly if the client shows the effects of what I'll call my negative intervention. And I'll alter my intervention in the next session or with the next client, based on this feedback. In this way, the failure narrative operates from session to session as a continuing feedback loop to correct some of what I think are my excesses or deficiencies.

JEANNE: I keep on wanting to differentiate between errors and failures.

MARNY: I see errors as part of the failure narrative, as a counter-narrative within failure. Often therapists perceive errors as second chances or as grist for the mill. This redemptive opportunity offered by our mistakes is illustrated by a great little poem by Antonio Machado, a Spanish schoolteacher:

> Last night as I was sleeping
> I dreamt–marvelous error!–
> That I had a beehive
> here inside my heart.
> And the golden bees
> were making white combs
> and sweet honey
> from my old failures.[3]

One way we convert failure to a blessing, the way we protect ourselves from too much ego damage, is by telling ourselves that ultimately we learned something, something was transformed, it was "a growth experience." I think therapists have to protect themselves from the failure narrative at the same time they are shaped by it.

NATALIE: There are pros and cons to that narrative. It is a way of seeing life and/or therapy in process. It is the idea that we are unfolding and becoming and learning and growing. But I wonder whether the flip side of this is that it makes everything value neutral. There are certain errors I am not neutral about, as when a therapist is too impulsive, willful, selfish–is intentionally dealing negatively with a client.

MARNY: But therapists would never admit to dealing with clients in intentionally hurtful ways . . . even to themselves. Or if they did become aware of acting out hostile impulses toward their clients, they would start to blame themselves. In other words, they would be caught up in the failure narrative. Let me give you an example of the feedback loop effect of the failure narrative in my own practice. A few weeks ago a couple came in;

one of the partners was very depressed. She was doing sales work. She was having to make cold calls to potential customers. Instead she complained about "staying home and doing nothing." I jumped in and said it was very important that she have more structure in her life and that the sort of amorphous sales work she was expected to do was probably bad for her depression. She said, "I'm feeling somewhat ganged up on, here." I still insisted and pushed the point that she needed more structure in her life. The couple did not come back. I realized afterward that, because I had been anxious about one partner's work situation, I had been much too directive. I felt like a failure. It was that feeling that caused me to be more tuned in . . . listening and refraining from unwanted advice . . . in subsequent sessions with other clients. I believe the failure narrative keeps rebalancing my work. I can err on the side of being a friend, a bossy friend who knows what is best for the client; or else I can be too cool and detached. My own failure narrative compensates for some of my excesses in one direction or another. I think the failure narrative brings me back to the center between these two poles.

NATALIE: From my perspective, you're describing the ideal outcome of the failure narrative, that when we receive feedback from our clients we correct our course in therapy. I don't define those events as failures unless they're very egregious. We do make mistakes; we err in one direction or the other. Our ability to use self-reflection to correct ourselves after receiving feedback is part of the process of continuing to grow as a therapist. What concerns me is when people are impervious to the process that you just described and blame the client rather than self-reflecting. In the example you gave, some therapists might interpret your client's decision to not return as resistance; another would be a client's refusal to get medication, as in Gloria Rose Koepping's paper in this [volume]. The therapeutic failure, in my opinion, would be when the therapist is impermeable to the feedback that one should use for correction. The therapist, however, may not recognize their own limitations as "failure."

WHEN THE FAILURE NARRATIVE MAY NOT BE HELPFUL

JEANNE: One problem with the failure narrative is that the fear of failure and the fear of the power can also lead the novice therapist to rely on "doing no harm." This stance may be tantamount to doing nothing. She may thereby relinquish her responsibility to keep in mind the client's goals that the therapist has agreed to support, too afraid or uncertain how to facilitate movement in that direction.

NATALIE: One way of thinking about the mixed benefits of the failure narrative is that we may tend to externalize what the problems are if we don't have such a narrative. We may blame our clients for their lack of progress in therapy without examining the role we played. This can happen either because we have not sufficiently bought into, or have risen above, our own accountability or because the failure narrative induces shame or humiliation. In the example that you, Marny, just gave the feedback rebalanced what you were doing in therapy. For others, the same feedback might produce more of the same behavior, in effect a counter-productive behavior. So while you talk about your rebalancing as moving from being too intrusive to less intrusive or regaining empathy for the client, similar feedback could create greater passivity in a passive therapist, rather than rebalancing toward more activity. If the therapist was being ineffectively intrusive she may become angry and even more intrusive.

JEANNE: And blame the client.

MARNY: Perhaps saying that the client wasn't motivated. Or the client just couldn't tolerate this sort of intense contact with somebody else.

NATALIE: Or the therapist may engage in some manipulative kinds of therapy. This is where I think some therapists misuse strategic models and provide paradoxical tasks, for example, in ways that are highly deceptive. That comes out of a failure narrative in which they're blaming the client.

MARNY: A displaced failure narrative.

JEANNE: I suspect that superficial "success" in sessions may lead to failure over a full course of therapy, whereas intermittent lapses of respect, of empathy, of authentic presence, or of honesty on the part of the therapist, if well handled afterward, may actually contribute to the success of the therapy process.

MARNY: Would you want to elaborate on that?

JEANNE: Errors of the kind I have just mentioned, specific errors at specific times, are *instances* of "failure." They're usually not even recognized by the therapist when they're happening. If I know I'm having a failure of empathy I will do my best to correct it right then and there–reach into my inner being and pull forth compassion, empathy, or at least respect.

However, I can disrespect the client and not be aware that I'm doing so. If the client reacts with anger, or even some other reaction, we can repair the interaction. We can make it into something good because the client has noticed what the therapist has not.

MARNY: You're saying that what we can call therapy errors are sometimes disconnections in the moment-by-moment interactions we have with clients. The client may have keenly felt the rupture, and has let us know it. We have the opportunity to either clarify or correct or reconnect with the client based on their feedback.

JEANNE: And say "thank you."

MARNY: Or say thank you. What you're suggesting is that in the long run those kinds of interactions . . .

JEANNE: Are good for both the client and the therapist.

MARNY: Interactions can be a corrective and therapeutic process in and of themselves, having those kinds of interactions between the two individuals.

JEANNE: Thank you for making it clearer.

NATALIE: Is it your perspective, that there is no success without failure– that therapy is comprised of many moments of failed attempts at making contact?

JEANNE: No and yes, but I wouldn't say there is no success without these "failures." The important part of them is that the therapist not disclaim them or be defensive when they are brought up by a client. When we know it ourselves and can bring it forth, that's the easy part.

Another part, which I think is equally important, is that *superficial* "successes" represent failure of the process, because we are not fully engaged. We have a too-easy agreement between client and therapist. Sometimes that happens when the therapist is talking too much.

MARNY: Still I go back to your saying therapists shouldn't be defensive. But then again, what if the therapist is defensive and then the client says, "You're defensive," and then the therapist says, "You're right, I am being defensive."

JEANNE: It's the friction that's productive.

MARNY: Yes, I would call it "productive" rather than a failure or success. I like that framework very much. I do think that part of the failure narrative is that we're all instructed that we must be authentic and we must be honest, and so on. This is where I take issue with you, Jeanne. I say that is really just part of the training of us therapists: to be authentic. Those are part of the conventional notions that go with the narrative of failure.

JEANNE: I'm not talking about the need for perfect honesty or authenticity or empathy or respect. I'm talking about doing and being the best we can, knowing that we are not going to be perfect–sometimes perhaps saying in response to a client, "I'm feeling pretty defensive right now. Let me sit with this for a minute." Then we move on as well as we can.

MARNY: Jeanne, what you are bringing up suggests that there may be conflicting failure narratives based on the therapist's theoretical orientation and perspective. What one therapist may view as a positive outcome, another may see as negative.

NATALIE: Yes. For example, those of us who have been sensitized to be empathic when a client is speaking of some intense experience, will be very very quiet, will listen carefully and try to maintain as much quiet contact as possible, so as not to interrupt the feeling being expressed. Other therapists, when something very powerful is happening–perhaps body therapists who believe in discharge–might behave quite differently and in a way that would seem distracting and invasive to the previously-described therapist. So, as we have agreed, the notion of failure in therapy is a very relative concept.

JEANNE: That example highlights one of my major concerns about relying too strongly on a failure narrative: the decision about what is failure or what is error appears to be the therapist's rather than the client's decision. Or what makes a good session or a not-good session.

Also, I'm finding myself chafing at the concept of the failure narrative because it is impossible for me to deal with issues of failure until I have some idea of what success is. To the extent that "success" is elusive of definition, then "failure" has to be equally elusive.

MARNY: I love that.

JEANNE: For example, Ellen Cole's paper shows clearly that in a situation 15 years earlier she'd known what she was supposed to do to resolve her dilemma. After careful assessment, she risked taking the less safe direction. As a result, she lost a friend.

MARNY: She invites her students to tell her what she should have done or what they would have done, to question and differ from her as she continues her anecdotal description of the circumstances. She tells them that "now" she should and would proceed differently.

What she did then was, after careful assessment, risk doing what she was not supposed to do. Among other results, she experienced much embarrassment in her community and lost a friend.

One might reasonably call this a therapy failure, but it is important to remember that the client couple originally came to her with their goal being to improve and continue their relationship. On that basis, the therapy appears to have become–ultimately–successful: the couple reconstituted their marriage not too long afterward and continue to send annual greeting cards to the therapist, still together after 15 years.

A "difficult case," certainly, but: a failure or a success?

HOW DOES "THE CONTRACT" FIT
WITH THE FAILURE NARRATIVE?

JEANNE: This is one of the places where the issue of "the contract," the implicit if not the explicit contract, should be considered. If a prospective client contacts me saying she is looking for some problem-solving therapy, I will not dispute that problem-solving is therapy. I will listen and say, "What are your concerns?" When I've heard some of it, I will often say something like, "Let's talk about possibilities, and what I may be able to do to help you. The concerns that you're raising may be such that three or four sessions of problem-solving will be helpful enough. On the other hand, three or four sessions of problem-solving may reveal deep-seated or long-standing issues now uncovered but not yet really addressed. In problem-solving we will have a lot of verbal interchange between us. I'll feel free to make suggestions to help you find solutions. If everything works well you'll feel resolved and therapy will be over. If, however, deeper issues have emerged–you may want to continue now, or return later, or go elsewhere. It would be a different kind of engaging, would take longer, and my behavior in sessions would probably be different. It will always be your decision." That's what I mean by the contract as a context for considering whether therapy endings are timely or "premature."

Can I keep talking? A man called recently saying, "I have an eating disorder." I bit my tongue and kept to myself, temporarily, my feminist opposition to the sound of "eating disorder"; instead I asked, calmly, "How do you define your eating disorder?" "I eat more than I want," he said, "and I don't like my body as a result. I'm fat and I don't feel attractive." I told him I have no particular training in eating disorders, and that it's a term I'm reluctant to use, but I was willing to work with him on issues of his feeling he eats too much, and on fat oppression, if it's relevant. I then proposed, as I usually do, meeting to find out if we will do well to work with each other. I was rather skeptical. When we met, I saw at once that he is not *fat*. He is a mid-sized person who would like to be thinner, and who exercises regularly and vigorously. After we had talked for about 30 minutes he told me that what he really wants is to be loved. This helped me to say, "You've given me two sets of things, one in one domain of therapy and the other in another domain of therapy. What I think we should do is move a little at a time on each of them, not ignore one and not ignore the other."

We agreed to four sessions, at the end of which he asked to continue for another month. I offered behavioral modifications concerning eating more than he wants to, and we used some dreamwork to approach both early-life issues and self-image fears.

During one of the early sessions, I had asked him what he sees when he looks in the mirror. "I *never* look in a mirror," he answered. "The mirror is my *enemy.*"

At the sixth session, he arrived beaming. "I did it," he said. "I looked at myself in the mirror, really looked at myself, and did not hate myself, can say I almost liked how I looked." We spent the rest of the session developing the implications of his experience, I think to our mutual satisfaction.

At the eighth session we spent most of our time exploring the decision he had already reached that it would be his final session. I asked about his wanting a lover, and he answered that he's feeling able to love himself, definitely does not want anyone living with him at present, *would* still "like to have a boyfriend." We explored potential setbacks and what to do about them if they occur. I asked if he had gotten what he came for, and he said, "Yes, and more." After a pause he added, "I'm going to miss you." I asked what about me he would miss, and he said something about my being "funny," implying witty, as well as having "so much wisdom." I let him know that if he should feel the need he would be welcome to return.

On terms of depth therapy, this client had just begun. On his own terms? "If life never gets better than this, that'll be *all right.*"

MARNY: A therapist will be trained in depth therapy and the client is really looking for some kind of problem solving or more concrete life help. Then when the client leaves, the therapist automatically assumes it's been a failure. In fact, the client may have gotten what she or he wanted out of the treatment.

I think you're suggesting a very interesting alternative to the success/failure narrative. You're proposing that therapists have a menu of modalities on hand. Depending on the client's wishes, you choose among them. If we're going to talk about alternatives to the failure narrative, I think this is a very nice one.

NATALIE: I think so too. The other thing it underscores is the role of power and the kind of power analysis a therapist should do. It seems to me that if the therapist has a set of expectations that labels as failure what clients want from therapy, because they don't want to go as far or do the things that the therapist thinks they should, that's really a control or power issue.

MARNY: Sometimes there may be parallel failure narratives between the therapist and the client. Still, it's very useful at times for one's own therapeutic narrative or success/failure to contradict that of the client. Take sex therapy, for example. Lesbians often come to me wanting to have more sex. Often I am not able to help them meet that goal. They are not having sex when they come in, and they are not having sex when they leave therapy.

JEANNE: And they don't change their goal.

MARNY: No. So we are all feeling like failures. The couple for not having more sex; me for not helping them. To get us all out of the not-good-enough zone, I have to figure out how to get rid of that god damn goal. Fortunately, sex *is* a very relative concept. It can mean anything from begetting children to disembodied fantasies. If I can show clients that "sex" per se does not exist . . . that they will have to invent their own version . . . then we have managed to set a new, achievable goal. In other words, my work with lesbian clients who don't think that their relationships are "real" unless they have sex, is to help deconstruct *their* failure narrative and reconstruct an alternative that attributes value to relationships that are loving, caring, and fulfilling even if they are not necessarily genitally centered.

ELEMENTS OF THE FAILURE NARRATIVE

NATALIE: I think now is a good time to talk about what elements go into a failure narrative, whether conventional or alternative–maybe a feminist failure narrative, which we will get back to later, will be different in certain aspects from a conventional failure narrative. Some of the conventional "failures" that occur to me– the no-no's, the "sins" of therapy in other words–include lack of empathy or attunement, boundary violations . . .

JEANNE: Or when the client doesn't seem to be changing in therapy, or if there's premature termination. Which reminds me often of premature ejaculation: one has had enough; the other is usually left unsatisfied.

MARNY: Or when my own psychological baggage somehow gets incorporated into the therapeutic process. In other words countertransferential issues I'm not aware of. Or not preventing couples or families from separating.

NATALIE: Perhaps we agree with some of those, and have our own definitions, too, of what we see for ourselves. Our own personal . . .

MARNY: Hot spots.

JEANNE: Well, one of the biggest for me is what I think of as taking the easy way out, not just once but over and over again. That can be telling myself I'm being "receptive" when I'm not actually keeping the process moving.

NATALIE: As we go through the litany of what we're trained to think of as therapy failures, what having a failure narrative does for some of us is to overdetermine our behavior in one direction rather than another. For example, if we recognize we are not attuned to a client, we may then overcompensate by being . . .

JEANNE: Too tuned.

NATALIE: Too tuned. Right. Or defining attunement as having a "feel good" therapy session.

MARNY: Or knowing better than the client knows what's good for her, an excess of attunement.

NATALIE: I was thinking of it more as related to what Jeanne had said about having therapy that's just going too smoothly.

MARNY: I see.

NATALIE: That's one of those where the therapist in some ways can pat him or herself on the back and say, the client is returning so we must be doing good therapy.

JEANNE: But that one is not in the conventional narrative. I was relating to the personal hot spots concept, and one of my hottest hot spots was a major boundary violation.

I violated client boundaries, mostly in my early years of practice, in the 1970s when so many feminist therapists–and other therapists too–were serious about fracturing old therapy rules but had barely begun to look at creating new standards. I still squirm at the thought of telling this particular violation, but it really does pertain to the concerns addressed in this [collection].

One of my clients had been part of a women's group I led; she sometimes also came for individual sessions. At the time she was about 20 years sober, sought after as an AA sponsor–a witty and wise woman, a lesbian. At the end of group or individual sessions she liked to hug goodbye. Her hugs were never sexualized, and other women kept the tradition going after she had left.

At one session–whether group or individual I don't recall–she had been working on some relationship difficulties. Her big question that evening was, "Why am I always attracted to unavailable women?"–one of whom she'd talked about during her work. When she came to me for a friendly hug, I did something I consider unforgivable: I asked her, softly even, "Am I one of your unavailable women?"

MARNY: While you were hugging her?

JEANNE: Yes, while she was hugging me. It was an outrageous thing to do! Imagine the double bind, too: how could she say either Yes or No without offending me?

MARNY: It's a wonderful example of what this discussion is about.

JEANNE: And do you know what happened next? After a moment's pause, she said in a straightforward way, "I don't think I want to answer that question." Those were her exact words. It seemed to me she had rescued me from disaster. I may have added something like, "Of course you don't have to answer it,

and I shouldn't have asked it"–something like that, or I may
have been mute. I *know* I was immediately grateful. But that
moment has lived with me for twenty years or so.

MARNY: It has made a big difference, since then. You thought it was a
terrible thing to do by your standards, or by therapy standards–

JEANNE: My standards. I was putting a client into a profoundly awkward
position, probably sounding seductive, perhaps *being* unconsciously seductive. I think I was still living a heterosexual life
at that time, not that *that* would have precluded anything.

NATALIE: That adds a context. Unavailable for that reason, not because of
your being a therapist, though that adds another dimension.

JEANNE: Our work together continued. We never spoke of this again that
I remember. I was too embarrassed, and I think she was too
smart, to ever bring it up. Therapy ended in due time, in a way
that seemed satisfactory to us both.

   When I called to ask her permission to include this material,
she said she didn't remember anything bad I had ever done to
her. She added that my telling her in the call that she had
handled it superbly, just about made her day. She didn't need or
want to have me read it to her, but asked that I send her a copy
of the [book] when it came out.

NATALIE: That's a wonderful example of a therapist's *big* error being
salvaged by a wise client–

MARNY: And becoming an apparently life-long correction. Do you now
refuse hug requests?

JEANNE: Rarely. Only when I really don't want to hug or be hugged. I
even more rarely initiate one. Even before I had thought very
much about boundaries, mine were clear to me. I thought of
them as carefully thought-out, flexible and even permeable,
but always present. But I certainly have not always made them
clear to others, to clients, nor had I in the early years been
aware how important it was for me not to trespass across clients' boundaries.

NATALIE: We're taught, especially these days, that we can get in terrible
trouble over boundary violations. It's good in a way but maybe

it doesn't stop violations, just frightens some people and maybe a little too much. They think, "If I create a boundary violation, I am going to get into trouble, so I am going to stand all the way back, be aloof and distant." The failure narrative does that to certain people. It might create a container not even a potted plant could thrive in.

You know, we had talked earlier about situations when the client and the therapist may hold different expectations about the goals of therapy or about their roles in therapy. I have found that with some clients I experience this difference as a failure experience whereas at other times I perceive the difference as not reflecting failure. For example, when clients come in with very clear expectations for how they want to change, which may differ from my judgment, but insist that it is my job to get them where they want to be, my own sense of inadequacy as a therapist is likely to be activated and I perceive the client's message as, "If you were only good enough, you could make this happen for me." I think these are the times I must monitor getting hooked into the failure narrative in a negative way. Of course, I can't meet the client's needs alone unless the client's working with me, but I may dwell on my inadequacies rather than on this reality. For me, this is an example of when the failure narrative message about the power of the therapist can result in grandiose thinking, on my part, on the part of the therapist.

Another example of this difference in expectations has occurred in my work as a child therapist. In child therapy, the parent may bring in a child saying, "My child has a problem." I may see the child's difficulty as related to significant problems the parents are having, but the parents refuse to engage in family therapy or participate in the therapy in any constructive way. Many times, the therapist can develop a relationship with the whole family and not just work with the child. Sometimes, parents who initially are reluctant to be involved may develop trust in the therapist when they experience that the therapist will not be judgmental or punitive toward them. They may agree to join the "team." But if parents refuse to make that shift and participate, I feel like a failure. I know that the issue for the child is never going to be resolved until the parents deal with whatever their issues are, but the parents are essentially saying, "I don't want to talk to you. I don't want to deal with this. Just treat my child." And I will not have created the conditions that encourage the parent(s) to participate.

MARNY: I just was wondering if that also ties into another therapeutic sin, which is not liking our clients.

NATALIE: It can.

MARNY: I think that's a big one.

NATALIE: That can happen particularly when I perceive that "what's wrong with the child" is emotional or/and physical abuse or a highly confrontational family environment that no one is willing to address.

MARNY: But what about even if you just don't like their personalities? They are perfectly civil and non-confrontational. You just don't like them.

JEANNE: One process that helps me get through an initial reaction of dislike is holding it within me for a while. That's why I like to start any therapy contract with approximately four sessions. If they can't afford to come once a week I even cut the fee in half so they can come once a week to get started. What I have learned in these years is that it doesn't take long before I find out why I don't like the client. Usually it is something of myself I have to "own." That's when I can start by respecting the client's wish to change and fear of changing, and the dislike diminishes. On the other hand, if it continues or gets stronger after three sessions, then at the fourth I can discuss things with the client: "I'm feeling that we're not the right persons to work together. I'm not the right therapist for you. Would you like some referrals or do you want to find others on your own? What do you think? Do you think that you would want to continue if I weren't saying this? Is there some way you see this differently?" I just put it out there early in the fourth session.

NATALIE: When I find myself not liking a client, particularly in couples or family therapy, it is sometimes because of the negative attributions about the motivations underlying their behavior. Reframing the client's actions or motivations helps me to salvage therapy at these times. I find it is one of the structural family therapy techniques that has been very helpful for me in reconnecting to an empathic understanding of my client. Even when the reframe feels contrived at first, I find it helps open me up to new insight, broadens my understanding of what may be motivating a client's behavior. When I can shift my own perspectives about why a client is doing certain things, I may both understand and like my client more.

MARNY: These techniques that both of you are talking about are wonderful techniques but they are still responses to an internal failure narrative of therapy. We have a hard time saying, I can dislike this client and still work with this client, which is outside of the conventional paradigm. I think this illustrates our point in some way. Even though I have no quarrel with these approaches, I still think they are emblematic of the failure narrative.

NATALIE: I completely agree. The internal failure narrative may even fuel my dislike because it is less uncomfortable to blame the client than to feel like a failure.

The ways I perceive the quality of a relationship with a client may also affect when I perceive a particular outcome as reflecting therapeutic failure. At times, I have found that I interpret similar events, such as leaving therapy earlier than I would like them to, in different ways. In one case I might feel like a "failure," whereas in the other case I would not. I think this perceptual difference is only partly about the matching of expectations; for me, it has more to do with whether I feel liked and accepted by the client. My own failure narrative also tells me that my reactions should not depend on needing to feel liked or accepted by my clients, so this is one part I don't really like owning up to in a professional journal!

Two examples came to mind. In the first case I had been engaged in individual therapy for over a year. The therapy was going well, seemed successful and I felt the client and I had a good relationship. She came in one day to say she was leaving therapy with me to go and work with another therapist in another type of therapy. I didn't want her to leave. I thought our work was not finished. I believed she was leaving to enter a questionable therapy practice. This client was a lesbian and had gone to a workshop that a very high status lesbian woman, who had just returned to the community, was giving. To me the therapy seemed fringey and not what would be useful. In this situation I did not feel unsuccessful even though her leaving fell into my typical "early termination" failure narrative. I understood her behavior as a step the client felt she needed to take, to assert her independence. I viewed her leaving in terms of her transference issues.

MARNY: I think the way you turned her termination around was really interesting.

NATALIE: One could see my interpretation as totally motivated by self-protection. But I felt very comfortable with my perspective the whole time and that it was important not to attempt to dissuade her or pathologize her because of her decision, or to impugn the other therapist or therapy. So, I never told her how I felt about what she was doing, but I did make it clear that I would be there and that she could come back to me at any time. In a month she did return.

MARNY: How do you think you would have felt if she hadn't come back?

NATALIE: At the time I wasn't at all certain she would come back, and it still felt okay. I felt we had done a lot of good work together and maybe she needed to go on.

MARNY: And maybe this is the key phrase. You felt like you had done a lot of good work, so you could let her terminate and not be a failure. If I see a couple just one time and they don't come back, I feel that I have failed somehow. I have no track record of good work with them to fall back on.

NATALIE: It was also about how I perceived the *quality* of our relationship. Whether or not that should matter, I am not sure, but I didn't feel threatened by her leaving. This is a big contrast to how I sometimes feel in family therapy.

The second example was where I did feel like a failure although the therapy was ostensibly progressing. I was treating an anorexic young woman and her parents. The mother had read everything on anorexia. She put every statement of mine under the microscope, because she believed I was going to blame her for everything. She interpreted all of my interventions as criticizing her and simultaneously I felt criticized by her. Any intervention I recommended that involved her or changed her role vis-á-vis other family members was met with her blaming me for blaming her. The therapy was more emotionally draining than usual and I questioned my statements, my motives, my adequacy. I considered it as a "failure" much of the time and my failure mantra played: "This is going terribly, I can't seem to forge another kind of relationship with this mother." I took a great deal of responsibility for this lack of "attunement" with her. The therapy was successful in the long run, but painful in the short run. I think part of my feelings of inadequacy were due to the conventional failure narrative and part related to my unresolved issues with my own mother, my own countertransference issues around maternal criticism.

MARNY: You were aware all along the way that you were not connecting?

NATALIE: Yes, but as it triggered my own feelings I grew more passive and compliant to what the mother wanted done rather than honestly telling her what I thought. I was feeling angry and criticized and wanted to withdraw. For me to work therapeutically and effectively I had to remain assertive and active, behaviors that were contrary to my emotional reactions and desire to be self-protective and conflict avoidant.

JEANNE: And in that very countertransference that you are talking about, you began doing to that mother, or you avoided doing to that mother, what you perceived her doing to her daughter as well as to you.

NATALIE: Initially, I think I re-created the same dynamic with her as she had with her daughter, including being alternately overly avoidant and overly intrusive. I recognized these tendencies and did remedy my reactions, but the failure narrative played on.

MARNY: As a therapist it was up to you to rein in the mother, and in actuality that was hard for you, to confront your mom. A ticklish situation. I don't remember a time when I had such an experience, but I'm sure I have. Fortunately for me I've safely forgotten it.

NATALIE: Not control the mother per se, but help the family change some interaction patterns that weren't working.

MARNY: But you had a failure experience during therapy but afterward a success experience. It is so fluid.

NATALIE: And even when, on a cognitive level, on some external criteria, I knew that progress was being made, I felt like a failure because of the "lack of attunement" I experienced. I think this also activated my feminist failure narrative: "I am supposed to be non-blaming to women and to mothers, and this mother feels blamed by everything I do."

JEANNE: In both instances ultimately there was success, but so very different along the way.

MARNY: I want to mention another therapeutic sin, another element of the failure narrative; fostering client dependence, otherwise known as interminable therapy.

JEANNE: True, but "interminable therapy" does not always result from fostering dependence. Maybe this is a good place to bring in the issue of resistance, and how it does or doesn't fit within the failure narrative.

THE FAILURE NARRATIVE INVOLVES RESISTANCE

JEANNE: Depending on the theoretical model someone is studying, being trained in, or supervised by, the beginning therapist will learn either that *resistance* is an unconscious repression of what would bring about essential insights and ultimately change–or that resistance is a relatively conscious process in which the client foils every attempt by the therapist to help the client grow, improve, get better, become self-affirming, or whatever the goal might be.

What is much less frequently taught is the extent to which therapists consciously or unconsciously experience resistance to their clients' attempts to communicate with them.

MARNY: I like the idea of substituting therapist resistance for client resistance.

NATALIE: Therapist resistance may derive from having only an intra-psychic view of client problems, as if the world around us contributes nothing to the pain or distress that impels someone to seek therapy. I believe in the importance of a societal context. I feel angry sometimes at therapists who only address issues from a psychological context–

MARNY: A purely psychological context.

NATALIE: Yes, a purely psychological context regardless of what may be going on in the daily realities of the client's life. In their paper, Mary Ballou and Gretchen Schmelzer struggle valiantly to avoid this pitfall. I define ignoring the sociocultural context as therapy failure, but those who don't have this perspective won't understand how they contributed to the "failure." They may think something is not going right in the therapy, but they label it all as the client's resistance. Marcia Perlstein's paper . . . speaks of impasses in therapy. What she calls an impasse may be very close to what another therapist would call client resistance, but by framing it as an impasse she is willing to share in the responsibility.

JEANNE: Would it be useful to connect resistance to the failure narrative by hypothesizing that clients resist success in the therapy consciously or/and unconsciously and therapists' failure narratives lead us to resist therapy failure? In Rascha Levinson's paper, throughout the therapy she feared and felt that she was failing. She sought not just one but two consultations. In neither instance, however, did she follow the recommendations of her consultants. Rather, she continued to try to follow her intuition, a path of "unconditional love." Eventually, after the client had left, the therapist came to believe that while the therapy had indeed been difficult, it had also been at least partly successful.

MARNY: That's a very intriguing idea. Can you elaborate?

JEANNE: I know I am very resistant to failure, to the extent that I have had to be dragged through these discussions at times, unable or unwilling to "understand" why a good, solid therapist seems to feel like a failure when she or he has made even a serious mistake. But I can feel something shifting in me. I have read each article in this [volume] several times as we have been formulating a collective approach to them, and now I realize I have distanced myself from much of the content by saying to myself, "Oh I wouldn't do that"–"I wouldn't have let things go that far"–"Well, yes, that was difficult and painful but why would it cause her to feel like a *failure*, for goodness' sake" . . .

For example, Nanette Gartrell's paper seemed miles away from my experiences until I woke one morning from a dream that had brought back to me the memory of a long-ago client who had insisted she was in love with me and who was furious that I didn't return her love.

More recently I looked at Nanette's paper while considering resistance, and thought that maybe resistances in that therapy had been reciprocal, the client resisting the therapist's limit-setting, the therapist resisting the client's wishes to talk in sessions about topics *she* chose. When I have been a client, with my heels dug in, resisting as if I was defending my very life, very small interventions were more helpful to my process than any big breakthrough attempts. Early training in Gestalt Therapy certainly taught me I must never tell a client what she or he was thinking or feeling, currently or in the past. I devised a do-it-yourself reframing process something like this: "I want to try saying in a different way what I think you have been saying. Would it feel true to you to say . . .? If it doesn't feel true, then it's not the right thing, so forget it."

MARNY: Take what you want and leave the rest. Sounds familiar. Jeanne, you've just added another element to my personal failure narrative. Along with inauthenticity, excesses or deficiencies of empathy or attunement, there is the matter of therapist resistance to client perspectives.

JEANNE: Right now I want to go back up to authenticity, which I see as double binding for a therapist. Surely one objective for a therapist of a client who's doing depth therapy is that the client will develop her own authenticity and be able to express it and be present with it. The therapist, however, is supposed to be authentic right now, in each session, but all the while maintain awareness of the behavioral constraints on the ways in which her authenticity is expressed. If I am angry, I must be careful to avoid acting out. So-called "negative" feelings must be expressed very carefully. If I am bored enough I have to find a way to deal with my boredom rather than lay it on the client. If something else is going on, whatever it is, I have to recognize what's happening within me and pull myself back into being present. In other words, there are behavioral constraints that limit the authenticity I can *exhibit* at any given time.

MARNY: I think that's where the failure narrative comes in again. It's constantly operating. Did I say too much? Did I say too little? Did I express too much? Should I somehow go internal with that feeling and come out with something else in a refined way? Not just pure anger or pure boredom?

JEANNE: But to do that during the session is to go crazy. If you're talking about after the session has recently ended, that's one thing. But in the session I think the only recourse the therapist has is to stay aware of her imperfection and treasure it. I didn't learn to treasure imperfection from therapy, I learned it from life–but it is an important element in how I work with clients.

NATALIE: That's a wonderful way of reframing the failure narrative.

JEANNE: My first conscious lesson came some twenty-five or thirty years ago. I was considering buying a very small oil painting by an artist who was a friend of mine. It was small enough for me to consider buying it . . . But it had one spot of color that was more conspicuous than the rest–it just stuck out! I thought, either this is what makes the painting or it is destroying its essence. I couldn't decide which. I mentioned my ambivalence to another artist friend who told me very solemnly that in every painting there is, and must be, an imperfection. I decided to buy the painting, went to the gallery, and learned it had just been sold. The second lesson came when some expert told me that Guatemalan weavings and embroidery all have imperfections because the belief in their culture is that only God is perfect.

What I do in therapy sessions is let people know that I'm not perfect, don't want to be perfect and that I treasure my imperfection. I tell them that I can't do good therapy if I try to be perfect, because then I would never take risks . . . the sort of calculated risks mentioned in the article by Marcia Hill, Kristin Glaser, and Judy Harden. Years ago I created a motto I tell clients is my motto. It is a wonderful mixed metaphor: "Imperfection is the salt of the earth."

MARNY: That's very funny. I love that mixed metaphor. Perfect and imperfect in many ways.

A FEMINIST THERAPY FAILURE NARRATIVE

NATALIE: For me, the feminist failure narrative includes my inability to integrate these issues about oppression, racism, sexism, anti-semitism, classism, etc. into therapy. Another measure is whether or not I have helped a client achieve some sense of community with other women, other people of color, other lesbians, etc. For me, successful therapy is when clients begin to see themselves as part of a larger picture, or develop a socio-political context for what is going on, and/or identify themselves as part of a larger social justice community rather than focusing solely on individually oriented goals. So my inner supervisor is looking to see at what level I've been able to introduce those kinds of issues.

MARNY: An interesting point that comes up when you describe those issues is that, in a sense, they are an indictment of conventional therapies. The items you just mentioned belong to a larger failure narrative than one sees in conventional therapy. These absences–the invisibility of women, of disabled women, of women of color, of lesbians, of a socioeconomic context, of a cultural context. This makes me think that new or alternative therapies derive from the larger narrative failure partially in opposition, but also as supplementing–we don't throw all of them out the window. We make the differences a basis for reinventing our own feminist alternatives.

JEANNE: Who do you mean, *we*, and *our*, white girl?[4]

MARNY: Oops! Point well taken.

JEANNE: The risk that's inherent in this is assuming that clients' values have to become more and more like the therapist's values rather than the client developing and being clear about her own values.

NATALIE: Right. In reality it may not be a failure if we don't address these issues. The client's values should determine the direction of therapy and not those of the therapist, the therapist's view of success or failure notwithstanding.

JEANNE: The real failure may be that the respective values are never looked at. If a therapist perceives her client as lacking in the areas that you're speaking of, not to even ask the client to explore her values and say what they are, how they arose, what they mean to her. And then be willing to say; "Well, we have a difference in values and I don't mind telling you mine if you ask, but they're mine, they don't ever have to be yours." I think we feminist therapists (as well as other therapists) unconsciously manipulate clients to adopt our values, which hinders a client from doing her own developmental work in that area.

NATALIE: Can we say that's part of a feminist failure narrative . . . to induce, entice, or coerce clients into our values? To me that ranks very high in a feminist therapy failure narrative.

MARNY: One of the things I'm struggling with is the apparent ways that what I've said and what you two just said may be seen as contradictions. On the one hand, I want to respect my client's values–not impose my values on them. On the other hand, I do want to expose them to feminist analysis, which may contradict their values.

JEANNE: They seem contradictory but they're complementary.

MARNY: Yes, and that's what I wanted to state here. I do think they are complementary rather than contradictions.

THE DISCUSSIONS HAVE TO END

NATALIE: This brings us full circle to some of the things we were discussing at the start about a possible difference between new and more senior therapists: for new therapists the failure narrative may be a stronger narrative. They feel that they have to be *in control* of the session, that they're totally responsible for what doesn't go right in the session, whereas more senior, more experienced therapists, are more likely to at least think we understand it's the process that counts and not the product. A younger therapist may be more product oriented. And I'm struck by the ways in which as *we* have had these conversations, in many permutations, one issue keeps coming back. When is this a way of protecting the therapists' self-esteem, shielding the therapists from real error, allowing them, ourselves included, to deny and rationalize–versus when is it an understanding of the process and that life is imperfect. Life *is* full of imperfections. Our job is to pick ourselves up, dust ourselves off, and keep going. Many of us as therapists have basically said that our imperfections are what allow us to work with the transference issues of our clients, because if they can see us as imperfect human beings and still accept us, neither idolizing nor villainizing us, it allows them to become more realistic in their other relationships.

JEANNE: So in some ways that does bring us back to what we said in the beginning, and also to what Natalie raised earlier. Is a failure narrative helpful or unhelpful. As Marny pointed out, there are pieces of both embedded in it. As for our imperfections, errors, and failures, when do they constructively help therapy move along. And when does this narrative become a way of buffering us from our shortcomings in ways that we don't even see.

MARNY: I think part of training should be, at least for students or interns, naming the failure narrative. Helping them understand that it's operating and having them look at the way it's operating in their practices, in their own evaluations of their clients and of themselves as new therapists.

NATALIE: One aspect we do poorly with trainees or students is that we inculcate the failure narrative in their work and a success narrative in our own work. They only see on teaching videos, and read in assigned texts, the successes of the masters. Meanwhile they're dealing with lack of success in their own work. It creates a big gulf filled with shame and humiliation in them.

MARNY: The negative side.

NATALIE: The negative side. It inculcates the negative side of the failure narrative and the ways the failure narrative may move them to become defensive and closed rather than open and flexible. Sometimes I kid with my supervisees that supervision makes me the perfect therapist because the supervisees tend to take credit for their failures and they give me credit for their successes.

MARNY: Ellen Cole's paper exemplifies this. She shared her failure with her students rather than her success, with very good results.

JEANNE: She shared her uncertainties, her misgivings, her *apparent* failure–but wasn't there ultimately more success than failure? I think the same is true of Geri Miller's paper. I still tend to think that the diverse schools of therapy try their diverse best to teach successful therapy according to their lights, and I am now finally convinced that what is *learned* is as little related to what has been taught as you, Marny, have spoken of the difference between what clients tell researchers was helpful, versus what therapists tell those same researchers.

As I've said, I really resist thinking of failure in relation to a course of therapy. Nanette Gartrell's clarity near the end of her paper was very helpful to me, however. "I am very disappointed," she writes, "that she left in a more disorganized state than the one in which she arrived." That clarity enabled me to recall an unarguable failure of a therapy relationship between myself and a certain client.

A year or more into therapy, the client wrote me an angry note (after canceling an appointment or two) saying how disappointed she was that "nothing had changed" though she "had tried so hard."

I answered with a note thanking her for hers and telling her I too was disappointed that more change had not occurred–that I too had tried my best. I invited her to meet with me one last time at no charge, if she wished to talk about this. I wished her well and reminded her that sometimes longed-for changes take place after therapy has concluded.

She then sent me another note, in an entirely different tone, saying that the "kindness" in my response to her anger had reminded her of how often I had been kind, that she appreciated my invitation but chose not to accept it, and that she most appreciated my continuing to offer her a sense of hope.

I never felt that either of us had done anything "wrong," or that she was leaving prematurely, nor was I glad she was leaving. I still consider this a kind of existential failure in which blame is irrelevant.

NATALIE: That would make a nice ending to the Trialogue.

JEANNE: The longer we three have worked with these concepts, the more it seems to me that the failure narrative cannot be re-ified, is not a *thing*. Rather, it is the result of attempts to educate and train therapists, promulgated perhaps even un-consciously, and then internalized, introjected, probably un-consciously, by the student or trainee. What has clarified this for me is a paper by Janet Lee in an earlier issue of *Women & Therapy* in which she describes a highly conscious process of feminist narrative therapy.[5]

And where I come to with it all is this: whatever "school" of therapy is being taught, it is taught as THE bedrock of understanding and practice–as, de facto, the ideal therapy theory, structure, and practice. In the course of such teaching and training, a failure narrative necessarily results, however (un)consciously. It is inherent because such teaching and train-ing describes conditions seldom encountered in the daily work of therapists. Fear of such failure is rarely absent from the minds and hearts of conscientious therapists, and probably lurks, deeply repressed, even in less self-evaluating therapists.

MARNY: Therapists' anxiety states derive from the failure narrative that is and has been an explicit and implicit part of virtually every therapist's training.

JEANNE: And as we finish, here, I've recognized something else. The failure narrative in therapy parallels a failure narrative in American society. If you are not a success on our terms, then you are a failure. I wonder if such parallels exist elsewhere.

NOTES

1. Edited and excerpted from an unpublished presentation to the Advanced Feminist Therapy Institute in Woodstock, Illinois, May 17-20, 1990.

2. Examples are: Garfield, Prager, and Bergin (1971); Strupp, Wallach, and Wogan (1964); Gillan (1971); Feifel and Eels (1963). Cited by Ellyn Kaschak in *Therapist and Client: Two Views of the Process and Outcome of Psychotherapy.*

APA, May 1978, *Professional Psychology*, pp. 271-277. Surely more studies of client/therapist pairs have been published in the 20-30 years since then, but these came readily to hand.

3. The poem appears at the end of an article by Katy Butler, "The Shadow Side of Therapy" that appeared in *The Family Therapy Networker* (November/December 1992, p. 15), published by the Family Therapy Network, Washington, DC.

4. Readers may remember radio and television programs about "The Lone Ranger," and his sort of right-hand man, a Native American Indian man named Tonto (a Spanish word meaning "stupid, foolish"), who addressed him as Keemo Sabe. In a popular anti-racist parody, the Lone Ranger and Tonto are surrounded by Indians. The Lone Ranger turns to Tonto and says, "We're in big trouble now, Tonto," to which Tonto responds, "What do you mean, 'we,' white man?!"

5. "Women Re-Authoring Their Lives Through Feminist Narrative Therapy," by Janet Lee, *Women & Therapy*, Vol. 20, #3, 1997.

A Feminist Model
for Ethical Decision Making

Marcia Hill
Kristin Glaser
Judy Harden

What is an ethical dilemma? By definition, a dilemma implies a conflict. Therapists make any number of ethical decisions over the course of a week, or even a day: to avoid revealing information about clients to colleagues or friends, to take a client's background into account in a therapy session, or to attend a workshop as a way of staying current in the field. Generally, these decisions are not experienced as dilemmas. Ethical codes as well as the therapist's moral principles serve as guidelines for behaviors that are well integrated into the therapist's professional identity.

A dilemma arises when the clinician experiences conflict, especially conflict that is not clearly addressed by one's principles or ethical code. Kitchener (1984) describes an ethical dilemma as "a problem for which no course of action seems satisfactory" and goes on to note that "the dilemma exists because there are good, but contradictory ethical reasons to take conflicting and incompatible courses of action" (p. 43). Any combination of one's values, ethical codes, the law, one's personal or professional loyalties, clinical knowledge, or personal feelings may come into conflict in a particular situation. For example, a therapist may have to choose whether to adhere to a legal requirement to report child abuse, knowing

The authors gratefully acknowledge the assistance and support of Michele Clark in the preparation of this section.

"A Feminist Model for Ethical Decision Making" originally appeared as a chapter in *Ethical Decision Making in Therapy: Feminist Perspectives*, Guilford Publications, 1995, pp. 18-37. Used by permission.

[Haworth co-indexing entry note]: "A Feminist Model for Ethical Decision Making." Hill, Marcia. Kristin Glaser, and Judy Harden. Co-published simultaneously in *Women & Therapy* (The Haworth Press, Inc.) Vol. 21, No. 3, 1998, pp. 101-121; and: *Learning from Our Mistakes: Difficulties and Failures in Feminist Therapy* (ed: Marcia Hill and Esther D. Rothblum) The Haworth Press, Inc., 1998. pp. 101-121.

that doing so will destroy the therapeutic relationship and may not ultimately protect the child. In such cases, the therapist must find a way to sort
through the variables involved, weighing consequences and prioritizing
values, in an effort to come to the best possible decision.

Ethical dilemmas are situations in which there is no "right" decision,
only a decision that is thoughtfully made and perhaps "more right" than
the alternatives. And, as every clinician knows, often the wisdom of a
particular course is not evident until long after the choice itself. For clinicians, an ethical decision is a particular subset of treatment decisions,
choices that affect one or more clients in the context of the therapist's
professional relationship with that person. Ethical decisions are treatment
decisions that in some way engage concerns about right and wrong, rather
than (or in addition to) other treatment issues such as effectiveness, timing,
or appropriateness of particular interventions.

When confronted with an ethical dilemma, a clinician needs more than
a code of ethics for guidance. She or he also needs some understanding of
how to use that code, as well as other resources, in order to come to a
decision that is "more right." As Welfel and Lipsitz (1984) state:

> Just as morality is more than a behavior that ends up helping or
> hurting someone else, ethics is more than the outcome behavior that
> conforms to or violates a code. The internal processes (intentions,
> motivations, way of cognitively structuring the ethically sensitive
> situation) are equally important. (p. 38)

This section reviews the literature on ethical decision-making processes, which covers intuitive and cognitive levels of reasoning and concrete models for ethical decision making, and comments on the limitations
of these guidelines and models from a feminist perspective. The second
section offers a more inclusive model for making ethical choices and
concludes with an application of the model to an example of an ethical
dilemma. This model for decision making is feminist in that the process
takes into account the emotional-intuitive responses of the therapist, as
well as the location of the therapist, client, and consultant in the social
context. Values, beliefs, and factors such as gender, race, class, and sexual/
affectional preferences of the people involved are assumed to affect the
various aspects of the ethical dilemma. In addition, this model includes the
client in the decision-making process whenever possible, which is compatible with the feminist principle that power should be made more equal
between the therapist and client when appropriate.

COMPONENTS OF AN ETHICAL DECISION-MAKING PROCESS

Moral Reasoning

Hare (in Kitchener, 1984) suggests two levels of moral reasoning when one is confronting an ethical situation: the intuitive level and the level of critical evaluation. The intuitive level is the way one first responds to the facts of a situation, the "ordinary moral sense" or the immediate sense of what to do, prior to reflection, and is based on beliefs and assumptions, including knowledge of relevant professional codes. There are some difficulties inherent in primary and exclusive reliance upon an intuitive level of moral reasoning, even though many ethical situations are simple and straightforward enough to resolve themselves quickly and without further deliberation. One concern is that intuitive thinking is permeated with cultural values, including values detrimental to women and other historically undervalued groups. In addition, reliance upon even an informed intuition can lead to a moral relativism that does not always result in sound ethical choices and that can be destructive to clients. The number of therapists who have defended sexual relationships with their clients as in the client's best interests (Rutter, 1989) provides one example of this concern. The limitations of intuitive moral reasoning make critical-evaluative reasoning, described by Hare (in Kitchener, 1984), necessary "to guide, refine, and evaluate our ordinary moral judgment" (p. 44). There are two aspects of critical-evaluative moral reasoning. First is the consideration of the basic and specific ethical rules, such as the Ethical Principles of Psychologists (American Psychological Association, 1992), or the Canadian Code of Ethics for Psychologists (Canadian Psychological Association, 1991). Second is consideration of the more general and fundamental ethical principles or higher-level norms (Beauchamp & Childress; Drane; both described in Kitchener, 1984) to which one can refer when the concrete codes are ambiguous, incomplete, or conflicting.

The basic and specific ethical rules consist of the appropriate professional code, laws, and case law. Thus, if a psychologist had a question about the appropriateness of barter, she or he would look at the new Canadian Psychological Association (1991) or American Psychological Association (1992) code of ethics and relevant casebooks, and a social worker would consider her or his own standards. One also needs to be aware of the state or provincial rules that govern the practice of one's profession and relevant provincial or state laws such as those that legislate mandatory reporting if child abuse is suspected. In some instances, federal legislation must be considered, such as the U.S. law that mandates equal educational opportunities for differently abled children. Finally, case law such as the *Tarasoff* (1976) decision concerning "duty to warn" has become part of the standards that professionals must consider. One needs to renew continually one's knowledge of standards, since they evolve over time and reflect changing professional values. For example, the new APA Code of Ethics adds rules about barter and reflects much greater concern with the rights of and protection of the consumer of psychology than the previous Code.

The more general and fundamental ethical principles described in Kitchener (1984) that form the foundation of this cognitive level of ethical reasoning in psychology include autonomy (the right to act as an autonomous agent, including the right to choice and privacy about that choice), nonmaleficence ("above all, do no harm"), and beneficence (promoting the welfare of others), justice, and fidelity (promise keeping). Nonmaleficence is considered by many ethicists (Kitchener, 1984) to be the strongest ethical obligation, to be given priority when two principles conflict, such as when a situation calls for both confidentiality and doing no harm, and doing both is not possible. Kitchener describes some problems and limitations associated with this level of reasoning, many of which she and the authors she reviews have addressed. One issue concerns the validity of the principles, whether they should be considered valid absolutely, only relatively, or in a prima facie way. Kitchener's review (1984) led her to conclude that ethical principles are " 'conditional' duties. . . . The conditions under which they may be overturned must, however, be morally relevant ones (i.e., when there are stronger moral obligations)" (p. 52). A second issue is the dilemma one faces when two or more of these principles conflict in a given situation.

Another problem inherent in the critical-evaluative level of moral reasoning that has not been addressed or resolved by the literature so far is that one's interpretation of the ethical codes, and the principles on which they are based, varies according to where one is located within a context of power (race, gender, class, etc.). Since the ethical principles are seen as fundamental to the more specific ethical codes of conduct, a look at some of these in terms of feminist principles will illustrate the nature of the problem.

All of the ethical principles reviewed here rest upon certain assumptions about those professionals making the decisions; one is that there is some common and agreed-upon sense of what constitutes harm and human welfare, and more significantly, that one's judgment about these principles is unaffected by one's personal and social context. The authors would argue that one's position in the culture, particularly in relation to power, deeply affects how one defines each of these principles and thus is at the very heart of one's ethical decision making.

Nonmaleficence, or "above all, do no harm," is ambiguous at its core in that what constitutes "harm to clients" is never defined. The authors argue that much harm has been done to female clients through the very nature of many theoretical models of psychotherapy that rely solely upon intrapsychic explanations of behavior and thus define human problems and their solutions in ways that blame the victim. Just a few years ago, women were frequently counseled to calm down and return to abusive situations, and they, rather than the perpetrator, were often defined as the problem. Such practices were considered not only professional, but well within specific ethical guidelines as well, and they have been harmful to women.

Similar concerns are associated with the principle of beneficence, since what promotes human welfare is equally ambiguous, and thus subject to influence by factors of culture and power. To the extent that women are viewed as "irrational" or otherwise "incompetent" by virtue of being women, to that extent can many acts of paternalism be committed "for her own good." For example, to the extent that marriage and heterosexual relationships are assumed to be the healthy norm, clients with other affectional preferences can be encouraged in a direction not in their best interests.

Kitchener also does not distinguish among different effects of ethical decision making depending on the particular characteristics of the client in terms of power. For example, in her acknowledgment of the lack of a clear definition of what constitutes harm, she describes the difficulty in determining "how much discomfort is justifiable in therapy" (1984, p. 48); she does not acknowledge that one's sense of discomfort can be exacerbated by one's relative power in the therapy situation. Exploration of an incestuous relationship by a young woman client with an older male therapist may have added layers of discomfort compared to exploration with a female therapist, where the power differential is not as great. Similarly, although Kitchener acknowledges the potential harmful consequences of diagnostic labeling associated with the medical model of mental illness, she does not address the differential impact of this labeling depending on one's racial or gender identification.

Models for Decision Making

The intuitive and the critical-evaluative levels of moral reasoning described by Kitchener (1984) provide a general background for the more concrete models of decision making, such as the ones offered by the

Canadian Psychological Association (1991), Haas and Malouf (1989), Jacob and Hartshorne (1991), Lafer and Lee (1990), and Tymchuk (1989). Haas and Malouf, in a very accessible general ethical guide, offer a flow chart for decision making. They illustrate the model, chapter by chapter, as they present ethical issues such as dual relationships, confidentiality, and so forth. The first step in the model is information gathering. The clinician first identifies whether there are one or more ethical problems. One must clarify who the "legitimate stake holders" are, particularly if insurance companies, hospitals, or guardians are involved. A decision must be made about who is the primary client and who has ultimate say. Finally, one must identify the applicable standards such as ethical codes, principles, and laws.

One enters the Haas and Malouf flow chart by asking if a single relevant professional, legal, or social standard exists for the question. If yes, and there is no reason to deviate from it, there is no dilemma, and one simply implements the recommended action. If no single standard seems apparent, one tries to identify the competing ethical principles and decide whether one principle is primary. If so, one seeks an appropriate course of action and implements it. If there is no clarity, one consults with others, researches the literature, and attempts to prioritize the principles. Where no ethical characteristic is primary, a variety of actions could be appropriate. The clinician brainstorms solutions, looking for answers that reconcile the competing principles or achieve a balance between doing the least harm and accomplishing the most benefit. The cost-benefit analysis is then applied to the various affected parties to see if the solution works for everyone. One also asks if the decision would cause any new ethical problems and whether the decision is both practical to implement and prudent for the practitioner. One then initiates the action and evaluates the outcome. Review and consultation are again recommended.

Haas and Malouf point out that the weakness of this model is that it is based on rationality and could therefore be used in a self-serving manner to rationalize poor decisions. The authors suggest that the assumption that this complex process ever could be strictly rational is erroneous. Most complex issues stir up feelings in the protagonists, and not to account for the practitioner's psychology is to leave out critical factors. The authors suggest a more complete model that is based on acknowledging both the rational and emotional components of an ethical decision-making process.

Additional Aspects of Ethical Decision Making

The literature about the ethical decision-making process, then, describes ethical codes, the general moral principles underlying those codes, and various models based on one or both of these guidelines. However, these approaches consider ethical dilemmas from a perspective that is almost exclusively cognitive and that gives minimal attention to the person of the therapist as a factor in the decision-making process. Ethical guidelines, as well as ethical decision-making models, look at ethical dilemmas objectively and from an intellectual distance. In actual practice, clinicians experience ethical dilemmas with an immediacy and personal involvement that cannot be completely separated out from their decision-making process. According to feminist principles, one's personal experience and involvement are legitimate and necessary factors to take into account in any analysis. In addition, ethical guidelines are of necessity generalizations and will therefore lack the complexity and specificity of any given ethical dilemma. As a consequence, it is understandable that most clinicians believe that they are not well enough informed to make ethical decisions (Tymchuk, 1986).

Situational or contextual elements in the particular ethical dilemma are missing from most ethical guidelines as well as from most research about ethical decision making; these elements are also a necessary aspect of a feminist analysis. Exceptions to this omission are Brosig and Kalichman (1992) who review the literature on child abuse reporting. They suggest that someone can only understand whether or not a clinician will report by looking at all the situational variables. They examine legal factors such as clinician's knowledge of the law and the specific requirements and language of the law; clinician characteristics such as years of experience, training, and attitudes; and situational factors such as victim attributes, type and severity of abuse, and available evidence. Similarly Lafer and Lee (1990) discuss the making of ethical treatment decisions with dying patients. In their examples they illustrate how the correct choice is unique for each patient based on her or his understanding of the illness, the characteristics of the staff, and the family context.

A book such as this one is also an effort to integrate the context into ethical guidelines. Although it is obvious that not all situations related to a given ethical issue can be addressed, specific examples may help the therapist better understand how the context influences the way in which ethical guidelines are prioritized and applied.

The person of the therapist has been strikingly absent from the public discourse on ethical decision making. It is perhaps this omission, more than any other factor, that has left clinicians feeling so inadequately advised about making ethical decisions. The omission itself is significant; what is not said often has as much meaning as what is said. In this case, what is implied by the failure to include the therapist in discourse about ethics? Does discussing ethics without discussing the therapist mean that the personal characteristics of the therapist (experience, culture, style, etc.) are or should be irrelevant to one's ethical decisions? Does it imply that the therapist's feelings about the ethical dilemma (intuition, countertransference, etc.) are or should be irrelevant as well? If guidelines are developed that do not include the therapist as a factor in decision making, then therapists who try to make ethical choices have guidance in certain aspects of the decision but no help in other aspects. By omission, therapists are implicitly instructed that certain factors should be ignored.

Some authors have looked at therapist characteristics as they relate to ethical choices without offering suggestions to therapists about how to take these factors into consideration. Kimmel (1991), for example, notes that "ethical decisions and moral judgments may be affected by the investigator's cultural and personal characteristics" (p. 786). His research indicated that clinician characteristics such as gender, years of experience, area of training, and employment setting were related to whether the clinician emphasized the benefits of research or the costs to the research participants in making ethical decisions about research. His study showed that clinicians who had held a degree longer, those with degrees in basic rather than applied psychology, those employed in research rather than service contexts, and male clinicians emphasized the benefits over the costs of research. Haas, Malouf, and Mayerson (1988), using a variety of clinical vignettes, showed that for some situations, therapists' ethical decisions differed by gender and years of experience. Brosig and Kalichman (1992) also show years of experience as being a factor in therapists' decisions to report child abuse. Welfel and Lipsitz (1984) state that a review of the literature finds conflicting results as to the effect of various therapist characteristics on their ethical judgments.

What is perhaps most useful to draw from the literature on clinician characteristics is the knowledge that it is likely that a therapist's personal characteristics (e.g., training, gender) will influence her or his priorities and values. Values are inherent in every work or training setting, as well as in every theoretical orientation, whether they are made explicit or not.

Time in a particular setting or working from a certain theoretical base represents at least a certain amount of exposure to specific values and often a personal investment in those values. Factors such as gender, ethnicity or race, religious background, geographic location, and so forth, are even more obviously related to values. The therapist's personal experiences of oppression and the uses of power (e.g., through race, sexual orientation, gender, size, disability, class, and age) will sensitize that individual in certain ways. Those same factors and others (such as religious background, family or living situation, or geographic location) will influence the therapist's priorities and assumptions. In order to make a feminist model for decision making, these aspects of who the therapist is cannot be separated from the decisions that she or he makes. If therapists turn to ethical decision-making models that do not address these factors, they then run the risk of making these factors invisible and thus not open to scrutiny.

The other general aspect of the person of the therapist that has not been included in models for making ethical choices is the psychological, a curious lacuna for a group of professions that claim expertise regarding the influence of the psychological on human behavior. Psychological characteristics of the therapist include those that might loosely be designated as countertransference, such as feelings about the client, the ethical situation itself, the process of consulting, and so forth, as well as personal characteristics that might best be ascribed to temperament or style.

Countertransference can include a range of feelings that influence the clinician's judgment in a given ethical dilemma. In the most traditional use of the term, the therapist might have feelings about the client or responses related to how closely the ethical dilemma touches her or his personal life. The therapist may also have feelings about her or his supervisor or consultant. More generally, there are the therapist's feelings about her or his competence, about the way in which she or he may have contributed to the ethical dilemma, feelings of responsibility or self-blame, or shame associated with the situation itself or with sharing it with a colleague. In examining an ethical dilemma, it is important that these responses be taken into account not only because they can get in the way of making a good decision, but also because they may be subtle indicators of aspects of the ethical dilemma that have not been fully considered. For example, a therapist may respond to a client's request for some special consideration by withholding and feeling guilty. Those feelings might be strictly personal, but they could also indicate that the request is inappropriate.

A therapist's temperament or style does not so much change an ethical decision as it shapes the form in which the decision will be carried out or fine tunes matters like timing or detail. A therapist with relatively high tolerance for anxiety may choose to wait and watch with an angry and potentially destructive client in a situation where another therapist might intervene more actively. A clinician with a more formal persona might be more inclined to avoid social settings in which clients are present, while a less formal clinician might address the boundary issues through negotiation and discussion with the clients involved. In any ethical decision, the therapist will find the most personally authentic solution if she or he is able to take these kinds of personal characteristics into account.

Another dimension not adequately addressed in the literature is the role of the consultant in the decision-making process. In the authors' experience, seeking consultation about ethical issues is quite common, even among very experienced practitioners. The consultant's values, conceptualization of therapy, and relationship to the questioner are likely to have significant impact. For example, depending on training and personal experience, one advisor is likely to have a more rigid or loose definition of boundary issues than another. In a different situation, an advisor would have a more distanced or impassioned reaction to the issue of reporting child abuse based on her or his personal experience with both abuse and reporting. Given that the therapist is seeking advice, or at least validation and reassurance about a dilemma, the characteristics of the advisor and the consulting relationship should also be scrutinized.

Finally, it is essential that the client be explicitly included in the ethical decision-making process as fully as is possible and appropriate. This position is informed by the feminist principle that power should be equalized between therapist and client to the extent compatible with good treatment principles. But perhaps more than that, inclusion of the client in the decision-making process is simply a matter of making the best possible decision. The client's perspective and reactions are valuable information that the clinician cannot afford to ignore. Sometimes, of course, not all those affected by a decision are available for discussion about the dilemma; occasionally, a client may not be competent to participate in such a discussion. In addition many aspects of any given situation are not appropriate to share with a client (most commonly, certain of the therapist's feelings, such as insecurity or shame or erotic feelings toward the client). Nonetheless, in most cases, the therapist can reasonably seek some form of collaboration with the client. Although clients may not be aware of the specific codes of ethics by which therapists are governed, they certainly are usually capable of understanding the general moral principles involved. The client's responses may well suggest factors or emphases in the dilemma that the therapist may not have considered. For example, a clinician might be trying to decide whether to accept for therapy someone who has difficulties that are outside the therapist's area of expertise. In this case, the therapist might be reassured to know that the client has other resources in that area or wishes to focus on concerns other than the area in question. In addition, even though the therapist carries sole responsibility for the ultimate decision, the perspective of the client should always be taken into account.

A FEMINIST MODEL FOR ETHICAL DECISION MAKING

A feminist model for ethical decision making combines the rational-evaluative model found in the literature (Canadian Psychological Association, 1991; Haas & Malouf, 1989; Jacob & Hartshorne, 1991; Lafer & Lee, 1990; Tymchuk, 1986), the emotional and intuitive aspects of the clinician's responses to the situation, awareness of the power difference between the therapist and client, and a recognition of possible cultural biases inherent in making value-based decisions. As feminists, the authors consider the inclusion of the person of the therapist in the description of the decision-making process crucial to making a decision that is more fully informed and less likely to be based on unexamined biases. Thus, the question "How does who I am affect this process?" is asked both emotionally and analytically throughout the course of making the decision. Although this model will be presented in a linear way, the steps may not always occur in this order, and certain steps may be repeated depending on the nature of the ethical dilemma. The actual process of decision making will weave back and forth between a more cognitive evaluation of the dilemma and attention to the clinician's experiential or feeling sense of the situation.

Recognizing a Problem

Recognition of a problem may come in any of several ways. Clinicians may simply recognize ethical problems from their experience and understanding of the therapy process or the ethical codes. Less experienced therapists may be informed by supervisors, colleagues, or clients. Frequently, the first indication that there is an ethical dilemma is the therapist's feeling of discomfort. It may be as simple as uncertainty concerning how to proceed in a given situation or may be complicated by other feelings. The initial task of the therapist is to identify any aspects of her or his feelings that stand in the way of understanding and sorting through the problem. One possibility is that the clinician has reactions to the nature of the situation that are not particular to the client involved. An example would be a therapist who knows that she or he is always a bit confused by difficult boundary dilemmas and tends to have trouble standing her ground when a client asks for special treatment in some way. Another general area of initial reactions that may be separate from the specific dilemma includes feelings that one may have about asking for help in examining an ethical decision. The clinician may feel that she or he should not have this problem, may feel exposed or ashamed for being in the situation at all, or may have feelings about her or his consultant. In any of these cases, the therapist may be able to resolve the difficulty before attempting to make the ethical decision. Alternatively, it may be enough simply to recognize that the particular feeling is an element of what she or he brings to the issue at hand and to mark it as something to stay aware of while going through the decision-making process. The decision to ask for consultation may occur at this point.

Defining the Problem

Now the therapist goes on to define the nature of the conflict. As previously described, a dilemma implies that there is more than one potentially right course of action. The therapist now asks, "What is the conflict?" in an attempt to identify what ethical principles, obligations, laws, or treatment imperatives may be at odds. The therapist identifies the people or institutions whose needs must be considered in the decision. Relevant standards, which might be formal ethical codes, general ethical principles, or laws, are also identified at this point.

Collaboration with the client is perhaps most critical during this stage of the decision-making process. The first step is for the therapist to determine the extent to which, consistent with good treatment principles, the client can be included in the process of sorting through the ethical dilemma. What perspective does the client bring to the therapist's understanding of the dilemma? How does the client define the problem? Both the rational and emotional dimensions of the client's responses may be explored.

In the emotional arena, the clinician can begin to use her or his felt experience as additional information about the ethical dilemma. Questions might include, "What else is my discomfort about? What do my feelings tell me about the situation? What am I worried about?" For example, a clinician knows that she should report child abuse that a client has revealed yet finds herself feeling very reluctant to do so. On reflection, she realizes that she does not trust the client's report and begins to consider her recent experiences with the client in this light, eventually wondering if the confession of child abuse were exaggerated in order to elicit a particular response from her.

Returning to the more rational aspect of defining the problem, the clinician at this stage would also take an initial look at the personal characteristics and values that she or he brings to the definition of the problem. This evaluation is particularly necessary if the clinician differs in any significant cultural way (gender, race, class, etc.) from the other players in the situation. It is important to ask oneself whether the client, for example, would define the problem differently based on cultural characteristics. For instance, the client may feel bound by cultural norms that the therapist cannot support, such as a particular attitude toward lesbians and gays or attitudes that significantly restrict options for women. These differences may lead the clinician into therapeutic, legal, or ethical conflicts. The therapist may feel that honoring the client's religious, ethnic, or other cultural expectations will ultimately harm the client. As with other conflicts, open discussion with the client and professional consultation are called for.

The decision to seek consultation may also occur at this point in the decision-making process. The therapist needs to be conscious and thoughtful about the consultant's personal characteristics and values and how they will influence the process. Under ideal circumstances, there would be open discussion between the two people about their influences on one another.

Developing Solutions

Now the therapist begins to generate possible options for responding to the situation. She or he will brainstorm possibilities and engage in a cost-benefit analysis of each option. Such an analysis is, in effect, an effort to address explicitly the primary ethical principles of nonmaleficence ("do no harm") and beneficence (do "the greatest good"). In addition, the therapist will consider whether the solution being considered is both practical and prudent (Haas & Malouf, 1989). Although the clinician may have already determined what factor in the decision is most important, in many cases the order of priority will emerge in this weighing-out process.

As she or he engages in a cost-benefit analysis, the therapist will also have intuitive or feeling responses to each of the alternatives generated. As described in the previous step, those responses are valuable information that can be used to refine further one's understanding of the nature of the dilemma and problems or benefits that may be associated with each possible response. Again, in many cases, the client can be appropriately included in the development of solutions. A fairly common example in small communities is the discovery that both the therapist and the client plan to attend the same social event. In discussing the dilemma, one or the other may offer not to attend or may suggest a way to interact that feels comfortable to both.

Choosing a Solution

The authors do not separate cognitive and emotional components in this step because the best decisions are made when both of these sources of information are included in an integrated way. The therapist asks, "Is this solution the best fit both emotionally and rationally? Does this meet every-one's needs, including mine? Can I implement and live with this?"

Reviewing Process

At this point, it is again critical for the clinician to ask how her or his values and personal characteristics might be influencing the choice of a solution. Once more, this questioning is especially important if the thera-pist differs from the client in some significant way. Would another clini-cian who is similar to the client in these dimensions make a different choice? Being in a position to make an ethical decision that involves the welfare of another person implies that one is in a position of power, and it is incumbent upon the therapist to look at how she or he is using that power. The "golden rule," which asks whether you would wish to be treated in this way, is a time-honored method to consider the rightness of a decision. The clinician might also ask her or himself whether the decision is universalizable (Haas & Malouf, 1989). Although every situation is unique, a decision that is too much of a special case may be a decision that is based too much on personal bias in some way. Haas and Malouf suggest that the decision be examined using the criterion of a "well-lit room." Does the clinician feel comfortable subjecting her or his choice to the scrutiny of others?

In a more intuitive frame, the therapist asks simply, "Does this feel right?" At this point, the clinician may wish to consider whether the specific form in which the decision will be enacted feels like a reasonably good match with her or his temperament or style. When time permits, it is often a good idea to sleep on a decision, to give oneself time to let any buried uncertainties or reservations emerge.

The therapist at this point generally communicates the decision to the client. When appropriate and realistic, the client can be asked to consider her or his reactions to the decision.

Implementing and Evaluating the Decision

Implementing the decision and evaluating the results are a unitary step in the decision-making process. The therapist carries out the decision while observing the consequences of this choice. Such action involves an ongoing reassessment of the ethical dilemma and the effectiveness of the chosen response. The clinician asks, "Is this the best I can do in this situation? Does my decision continue to feel right?" It is not uncommon for the therapist's intervention to throw more light on the situation, which might then lead to a redefinition of the problem, development of further solutions, and so forth.

The client's responses to the ethical decision are, of course, a primary consideration. When feasible and appropriate in terms of treatment considerations, the therapist may choose to include the client in the ongoing process of evaluating whether the decision continues to feel right or needs to be rethought.

Continuing Reflection

Every experience changes the people involved. After the ethical dilemma is resolved, the clinician integrates the experience in some way. Experience is valuable to the extent that it can be used to inform and enrich future understanding and choices. Cognitively, the therapist might consider what she or he learned from this situation. Are there things that she or he would do differently if faced with a similar dilemma in the future? More globally, the therapist asks, "How have I changed as a result of this decision?" For example, has this experience had the long-range impact of making the therapist more cautious about a particular issue or more sensitive in some area? This kind of self-knowledge may be part of what one brings to the next ethical dilemma.

Table 1 summarizes the steps of the decision-making process. The interaction between the rational-evaluative and the feeling-intuitive aspects of the model are also illustrated.

The following example illustrates how this model might be implemented in a clinical situation. Note that in actual practice one or several of the steps may need to be repeated as the clinician's understanding of the ethical dilemma unfolds.

AN EXAMPLE OF IMPLEMENTING THE MODEL

Recognizing a Problem

An experienced therapist had been seeing a quite troubled man in his early 20s for about six weeks. The young man described a history of difficult relationships, most often with himself in the victim role. He was having an affair with a significantly older, married woman. The client seemed satisfied with the relationship, feeling that he was finally safe. He had few concerns about his lover's married status because he spent as much time with his lover as he wished. The therapist had mixed feelings but was biding her time, since the client was focused on other issues.

The young man then reported that his lover, as a necessary part of her training, wanted to participate in an upcoming certification workshop conducted by the therapist. The lover had asked the young man to check it out with the therapist. The client volunteered that he had no problem about it, and the therapist agreed to think it over.

The therapist's immediate response was mild discomfort and a sense of confusion. After the session, she realized that there were several conflicting ethical issues. Because of the conflicting issues and her sense of discomfort, she sought a consultation with a colleague who had strong feelings about boundary issues.

Defining the Problem

The therapist outlined the conflicting ethical guidelines to her colleague. She was enjoined by her professional ethical code to avoid overlapping relationships whenever possible. However, she also was the only available certifying practitioner in her rural area and to refuse might mean harm to the lover. The consultant was concerned about the implications of developing a dual relationship with the lover and became concerned about treatment implications. Would her acceptance of the lover make it seem as if she were condoning the affair? Would it replicate the conditions of the triangle? Would her power position as giver of certification create transferential feelings in either client or lover? How else would getting to know the lover (or refusing her) affect her therapeutic work?

TABLE 1. Feminist Ethical Decision-Making Model

Rational-evaluative process	Feeling-intuitive process
	Recognizing a problem
Information from therapist's knowledge; advice from supervisor or colleague	Uncertainty about how to proceed in situation
	Identify what stands in the way of working through the problem: feelings about the nature of the issue, feelings about the consultant or about asking for help

(Decision to consult may occur here)

Defining the problem

What is the conflict? Who are the players? What are the relevant standards? (rules, codes, principles)

What else is my discomfort about? What do my feelings tell me about the situation? What am I worried about?

What personal characteristics and cultural values do I bring to this decision? How do these factors influence my definition of the problem?

How does the client define the problem?

What are the client's feelings about the dilemma?

(Decision to consult may occur here)

What personal characteristics, values does the consultant bring to this process?

How do the consultant's characteristics affect me?

Developing solutions

Brainstorm possibilities. Cost-benefit analysis. Prioritize values.

What do my reactions to each choice tell me?

Choosing a solution

What is the best fit both emotionally and rationally? Does this solution meet everyone's needs, including mine? Can I implement and live with the effects?

Reviewing process

Would I want to be treated in this way? Is the decision universalizable? Would this decision withstand the scrutiny of others?

Does the decision feel right? Have I given myself time to let reservations emerge?

How are my values, personal characteristics influencing my choice? How am I using my power?

Does the manner in which I carry out this decision fit my style?

Have I taken the client's perspective into account?

TABLE 1 (continued)

Implementing and evaluating the decision

Carry out the decision   Is this solution the best I can do?
Observe consequences
Reassess the decision   Does the outcome continue to feel
                                              right?
How has this decision affected
the therapeutic process?

Continuing reflection

What did I learn?   Have I changed as a result of this
                                              process? How?
What would I do differently?   How might this experience affect me
                                              in the future?

Note. From "A Feminist Model for Ethical Decision Making" by M. Hill, K. Glaser, and J. Harden (1995). In E. J. Rave and C. C. Larsen (Eds.), *Ethical Decision Making in Therapy: Feminist Perspectives*. New York: Guilford Press.

Developing Solutions and Choosing a Solution

The therapist and consultant first brainstormed to see if there were other options than acceptance/refusal. They could not find other alternatives. They then considered the primary choices: (1) Accept the lover and work through the consequences as they evolve. The consultant did not care for this solution. (2) Refuse the lover and work through the consequences with the client. The therapist would clearly avoid the overlapping relationship but might engage the client in a deeper level of transference than appropriate for the current stage of therapy. The therapist was not very comfortable with this solution, but it seemed the better choice.

Reviewing Process

The therapist continued to think the situation over for a few days, remaining unsettled about the choice. Partially she realized she felt pushed by the consultant, but there was another source of yet unidentified disquiet.

To gather further data, she discussed the issue again with her client. He gave the issue more thoughtful consideration but said that he did not feel any danger to himself. He trusted both his lover and the therapist. The workshop was brief, and he did not understand what the "big deal" was. His reaction led the therapist to examine her own sense of caution and wonder if she were reacting differently than the client because of gender. Perhaps for some men these kinds of overlaps simply were not "such a big deal." She also considered, and then discarded as not important here, the substantial class-of-origin difference between her and her client.

Rechoosing a Solution

The therapist sought a second consultation from her colleague. As they reexamined the material, they realized that another treatment principle was at stake. Not to honor the client's choice without compelling reasons would constitute a paternalistic response from the therapist. At this stage of treatment the therapist did not feel as though she knew more than the client did about what was best for him. The risk of harm was less than the risk of refusing to work collaboratively with him about treatment decisions and of refusing to let him have as much power as possible in the therapeutic relationship.

When the therapist considered the possible negative consequences of accepting the lover, she realized that at the worst it would stir up transferential responses that she believed she could handle. The consultant agreed with the choice.

Implementing and Evaluating the Decision

The "most benefit, least harm" choice was made to accept the partner in the workshop. The therapist had opened discussion with the client, and they would continue to discuss his feelings as the situation unfolded. The therapist also realized that the choice also suited her character. Even though she has no trouble holding her ground with clients, she did not relish taking a paternalistic stance unless absolutely necessary.

Continuing Reflection

Several months later, the therapist reported that the decision seemed to have worked well. The lover had maintained a professional stance in the workshop, and the client had been so deeply absorbed in other work that he seemed to have no further reactions. Given that the outcome seemed so benign, the therapist had been wondering why it had become such a "big deal." She decided that she must have been more stirred up about the client's affair than she had realized and had displaced that concern onto the request about the workshop. She was glad she had not settled for her first decision. She also thought she had learned a lot about the ethical decision-making process in general. Of particular interest to her were the facts that the obvious decision is not necessarily the best; that frequently ethical decisions have an evolving, unfolding quality; that supervision is not an unbiased process; and that when possible, consultation with the client should be central.

In considering this case, it is important to realize that were the situational factors different, the choice and outcome could also have been different. If the therapist thought the affair were damaging or she had recently experienced troublesome boundary issues, she might have kept her original decision. If the consultant had been in a more powerful supervisory position with a less experienced therapist, the original choice might have prevailed. If the lover turned out to be a difficult person or a poor student, the outcome might not have been so successful. Most ethical decision-making processes are relative to the people and the conditions of that situation. Assessing the situational correctness is as important as the reconciliation of underlying principles and rules. Full consciousness of all the variables allows a fully informed decision.

CONCLUSION

The focus in this section has emphasized aspects of ethical decision making that the authors have experienced clinically and that are consistent with feminist principles of analysis but have been missing from the literature. As a feminist, one must consider the emotional-intuitive responses of the therapist; the sociocultural context of the therapist, client, and consultant, particularly as it relates to issues of power; and the client's participation in the decision-making process. More work needs to be done regarding how factors of ethnic identification, affectional preference, gender, class, and so forth affect the prioritization of values. Guidelines about the extent to which the client could be included in solving ethical dilemmas would also be valuable.

REFERENCES

American Psychological Association. (1992). Ethical principles of psychologists and code of conduct. *American Psychologist, 47,* 1597-1611.

Brosig, C. L., & Kalichman, S. C. (1992). Clinicians' reporting of suspected child abuse: A review of the empirical literature. *Clinical Psychology Review, 12,* 155-168.

Canadian Psychological Association. (1991). *Canadian code of ethics for psychologists* (rev.). Old Chelsea, PQ: Author.

Haas, L. J., & Malouf, J. L. (1989). *Keeping up the good work: A practitioners's guide to mental health ethics*. Sarasota, FL: Professional Resource Exchange.

Haas, L. J., Malouf, J. L., & Mayerson, N. H. (1988). Personal and professional characteristics factors in psychologists' ethical decision making. *Professional Psychology, 19*, 35-42.

Jacob, S., & Hartshorne, T. S. (1991). *Ethics and law for school psychologists*. Brandon, VT: Clinical Psychology Publishing Co.

Kimmel, A. J. (1991). Predictable biases in the ethical decision making of American psychologists. *American Psychologist, 46*, 786-788.

Kitchener, K. S. (1984). Intuition, critical evaluation and ethical principles: The foundation for ethical decisions in counseling psychology. *Counseling Psychologist, 12*, 43-55.

Lafer, B. H., & Lee, S. S. (1990). A framework for ethical decision making with dying patients. *Psychotherapy in Private Practice, 8*, 69-82.

Rutter, P. (1989). *Sex in the forbidden zone*. Los Angeles: Jeremy Tarcher.

Tarasoff v. Regents of University of California, 529 P.2d 533 (Cal. 1974); 551 P.2d 334, 331 (Cal. 1976).

Tymchuk, A. (1986). Guidelines for ethical decision making. *Canadian Psychology, 27*, 36-43.

Welfel, E. R., & Lipsitz, N. E. (1984). The ethical behavior of professional psychologists: A critical analysis of the research. *Counseling Psychologist, 12*, 31-42.

Index

Adleman, Jeanne, 69
Anger therapy
   client description and, 55-56
   countertransference and, 59-60
   listening, value of, 61
   therapist anxiety and, 55-56,58
   therapist rejection and, 59
   uncared-for child, anger venting
     and, 56-58
   unconditional love, therapeutic
     value of, 57,58,61,92
Anxiety management, of client and
     therapist
   consultation issue and, 53
   family dynamic issues and, 51-52
   multiple diagnoses, problems of,
     50,52
   personal and career issues overlap
     and, 50-51
   pharmacotherapy and, 52-53
   social phobia and, 50
   summary regarding, 49
   of therapist, 50,52-54
Autonomy, in ethical reasoning, 104

Ballou, Mary, 13
Beneficence, in ethical reasoning,
     104,105

Canadian Code of Ethics for
     Psychologists, 103
Case examples
   of anger therapy, 55-61
   of anxiety management, 49-54
   of couples therapy, ethical-decision
     making in, 31-38
   of cross-cultural counseling, 41-47

   of eroticized transference, 6-11
   of ethical decision-making, feminist
     model of, 115-116,118-120
   of ethical decision-making,
     self-disclosure teaching
     approach to, 32-36
   See also Multiple issues, case
     example of
Childs, E. Kitch, 70
Cole, Ellen, 31
Conditional duties, of ethical
     principles, 104
Countertransference
   in anger therapy, 59-60
   ethical decision-making and, 109
   premature termination and, 64-65
   termination by client and, 67-68
   termination by therapist and, 65-67
   therapeutic failure and, 14,63-64
   therapeutic failure narrative and,
     90-91
Crisis, therapeutic failure as, 14
Critical evaluation level, of moral
     reasoning, 103-104
Cross-cultural counseling
   empowerment through, 46-47
   language barrier, effects of, 43-44
   referral possibilities and, 44
   suggestions regarding, 47
   summary regarding, 41
   Transactional Analysis use and,
     45-46
   translator use in, ethics of, 42
Cultural values, in critical evaluation
     level of moral reasoning, 103

Decision-making. *See* Ethical decision-
     making, *specific subject*

© 1998 by The Haworth Press, Inc. All rights reserved.   *123*

Haworth
DOCUMENT DELIVERY
SERVICE

This valuable service provides a single-article order form for any article from a Haworth journal.

- *Time Saving:* No running around from library to library to find a specific article.
- *Cost Effective:* All costs are kept down to a minimum.
- *Fast Delivery:* Choose from several options, including same-day FAX.
- *No Copyright Hassles:* You will be supplied by the original publisher.
- *Easy Payment:* Choose from several easy payment methods.

Open Accounts Welcome for . . .
- Library Interlibrary Loan Departments
- Library Network/Consortia Wishing to Provide Single-Article Services
- Indexing/Abstracting Services with Single Article Provision Services
- Document Provision Brokers and Freelance Information Service Providers

---

MAIL or *FAX* THIS ENTIRE ORDER FORM TO:

Haworth Document Delivery Service
The Haworth Press, Inc.
10 Alice Street
Binghamton, NY 13904-1580

or FAX: 1-800-895-0582
or CALL: 1-800-429-6784
9am-5pm EST

PLEASE SEND ME PHOTOCOPIES OF THE FOLLOWING SINGLE ARTICLES:
1) Journal Title: _____
   Vol/Issue/Year: _____ Starting & Ending Pages: _____
   Article Title: _____
   _____

2) Journal Title: _____
   Vol/Issue/Year: _____ Starting & Ending Pages: _____
   Article Title: _____
   _____

3) Journal Title: _____
   Vol/Issue/Year: _____ Starting & Ending Pages: _____
   Article Title: _____
   _____

4) Journal Title: _____
   Vol/Issue/Year: _____ Starting & Ending Pages: _____
   Article Title: _____
   _____

(See other side for Costs and Payment Information)

COSTS: Please figure your cost to order quality copies of an article.

1. Set-up charge per article: $8.00
    ($8.00 × number of separate articles) _____

2. Photocopying charge for each article:

    1-10 pages: $1.00 _____

    11-19 pages: $3.00 _____

    20-29 pages: $5.00 _____

    30+ pages: $2.00/10 pages _____

3. Flexicover (optional): $2.00/article _____

4. Postage & Handling: US: $1.00 for the first article/
    $.50 each additional article _____

    Federal Express: $25.00 _____

    Outside US: $2.00 for first article/
    $.50 each additional article _____

5. Same-day FAX service: $.50 per page _____

GRAND TOTAL: _____

METHOD OF PAYMENT: (please check one)

❑ Check enclosed ❑ Please ship and bill. PO # _____
    (sorry we can ship and bill to bookstores only! All others must pre-pay)

❑ Charge to my credit card: ❑ Visa; ❑ MasterCard; ❑ Discover;
    ❑ American Express;

Account Number: _____ Expiration date: _____

Signature: *X* _____

Name: _____ Institution: _____

Address: _____

_____

City: _____ State: _____ Zip: _____

Phone Number: _____ FAX Number: _____

MAIL or *FAX* THIS ENTIRE ORDER FORM TO:

Haworth Document Delivery Service | **or FAX:** 1-800-895-0582
The Haworth Press, Inc. | **or CALL:** 1-800-429-6784
10 Alice Street | (9am-5pm EST)
Binghamton, NY 13904-1580